DAD, THE DONKEY'S ON FIRE

Also by Ian McMillan from Carcanet

Selected Poems

Dad, the Donkey's on Fire

Ian
McMillan

CARCANET

First published in 1994 by
Carcanet Press Limited
4th Floor, Conavon Court
12-16 Blackfriars Street
Manchester M3 5BQ

A CIP catalogue record for this book
is available from the British Library.
ISBN 0 85635 806 1

The publisher acknowledges financial assistance
from the Arts Council of England

Set in 10½pt Garamond Simoncini by Bryan Williamson, Frome
Printed and bound in England by SRP Ltd, Exeter

Funded by
THE
ARTS
COUNCIL
OF ENGLAND

Contents

Acknowledgements are due to the following, where some of these poems and stories first appeared: *Walking the Dog and Other Stories* (Redbeck Press, 1986), *Northern Stories 2* (Littlewood, 1990), *Slow Dancer, Dog, Sheaf, Smoke, Sheffield Telegraph, Poetry Book Society Anthologies, The North, Klaonica* (Bloodaxe, 1993), *Poetry and Audience, BBC Wildlife Magazine, The New Poetry* (Bloodaxe, 1993), *Wide Skirt* and *Poetry Review. More Poems Please, Waiter,* and *Quickly* was published by Sow's Ear in 1988. *A Chin?* was published by Wide Skirt Press in 1991. Some of the poems and stories have been broadcast on BBC Radio 1 and BBC Radio 4. 'Snails on the West Shore, August 1991' won the BBC Wildlife Poet of the Year Award, 1992.

Kake Yourself Comfortable

Kome in. Sit Kown.
Kake yourself comfortable.

Kup of Kea? Bit of Kake?
Kilk? Kugar?

My problem? You Kish
to Kiscuss it?

Ah yes. The letter K.
Well, Kit all goes back

Ko Ky Khildhood. We were
very Koor. I only had one

Koy. A building Krick with
Ketters on. Except all the

Ketters had Keen Kubbed off,
except one. All my childhood

I Konly Kever saw Kone letter.
The letter S.

Why We Need Libraries

It is the mid-sixties, and it
does not matter which year exactly;

it may have been the year Mrs White
threw water on the cat. It may not.

At the bottom of the hill, opposite
the football factory which will close

in 1981 (although nobody knows this
because nobody can look into the future

in fact the future is a pair
of stout walking boots in a sealed box)

they are loading books from the old
library to take to the new library

which is near the new clinic and not
far from the new old folks' home

at the top of the hill. Yes, isn't
it symbolic that these new things are

at the top of the hill. Yes, isn't
that Ian McMillan and his pal Chris

Allatt waiting outside the empty new
library, the green tickets in their

fists, their eyes hungry for Biggles?
It is the mid-sixties, and the future

is waiting to walk away from us, briskly,
as though we smell funny, leaving the new

library to darken and crack into the old
library, closed on Saturday afternoons

Everyman I will go with thee and be thy
guide except on Saturday afternoons and

sometimes all day Mondays and sometimes
certain days for the need of money to pay

the people who open the doors to let the books
out. You never know what will happen, though,

because the future is a book in a private
library. Unless we can request that book

and borrow it and read it and read it.

Pit Closure as Art

In the centre of
the major retrospective
there is a door
which you open.

As you open it
certain nerves
in the face
are jangled
artificially:
you smile.

The smile becomes
the property of
The Artist.

Beyond the door
is a room
and another door.

You walk over to the door.

The catalogue says
'The door will not be locked'
but the catalogue also
is part of The Art.

The door is locked.
The door you came through
is locked. The Artist
has served The Art well.

As you stand there
certain nerves
in the eyes
are jangled
artificially:
you weep.

The tears become
the property of
The Artist.

You dig to keep warm.
The Artist arrests you for digging.
The Artist smashes your head
for pounding on the door.

The Artist prevents you
walking to the door.

All this is part of The Art.
The Artist has refined The Art well.

Lilian's Poem

A white box
with a bunch of violets on.
That's what I remember most.

The gaffer's name was Jones
and he wouldn't let you sing.
The girls liked to sing.

Nobody liked Mr Bowman.
He used to come and stand over you.
He stood over me.

A man came round every month
to put poison on the floor,
poison on the floor for the rats.

In the war men came to the door,
wanting their wives to come home,
wanting their wives to come home with them.

But I remember most
the violets
on the blue box.

(Lilian was a housebound woman I worked with when I was writer-in-residence
with Age Concern Leicester in 1987/8. The words are all hers.)

Death's Feet

I don't know. Sometimes you lie
and then you call it art. The man said
'Are you working on a novel?' and

I said, YES, O YES, YES I AM, YES.
And he said 'I hope it's one of your
Inspector McMillan novels. I just

love his jutting jaw, and the way
he solves it on the penultimate
page, leaving the last page free

for recipes.' And I said YES O YES
AYE AR THIS IS IT PAL AYE AR YES.
And he said 'Do you have a title

for it?' And I coughed and said
COUGH ER AR TITLE AR WELL THA
KNOWS SEMMAS COUGH ER death's feet.

come stalky stalky
up the path
feeling your tie
in the moon's pale light.

Husband and Wife

We had to move, you see,
to be near the husband's work.
Literally, the husband's work
has taken him all over the place.

I am happy though enough.
I can sit at the window
and see blackbirds, clouds.

The husband's work, you see,
we have to move with it.
This time, we moved into the kitchen,
last time it was into the shed.

He calls his thoughts
'A letter from head office'.
The husband bends over his work
making it scream.

Tempest Avenue

It is 5 am, and I am standing
in the half-light bedroom
holding our son. He is finally asleep

and I lay him gently in the cot,
trying not to rattle the toy bear
attached to the bars. Next door

Mr Lowe is having a dream about
the glassworks at Stairfoot. Look:
all the workers have turned to glass,

what a strange dream. Across
the road, Mr Ford is cycling
out of his drive to the pit. He

cycles during the week, takes the car
at weekends. Down the street
my mam is standing at the kitchen

window, looking at our house, thinking
'Our Ian will be asleep. I hope
Mr Ford's squeaky cycle doesn't wake him up.'

And I am being careful, so careful
with these words, laying them
gently into this poem, turning to the door.

Deaths from Ice Cream

Man killed by eating whole cone too
quickly. Woman died after slipping

on ice cream, falling under bus
carrying brass band. Child dies

sitting in snow trying to cool
dripping cone. Man killed by 99

hurled from hot air balloon by
lute player. Woman died after

argument with ice cream salesman
in Fife. Child dies of depression

after ice cream melts away. Man
killed by razor placed in ice cream

by crazed methodist. Woman died
after eating three hundred ice creams

for a wager. Child dies after
falling into a giant vat of ice

cream during factory visit.

Ted Hughes is Elvis Presley

I didn't die
that hot August night.
I faked it,

stuffed a barrage balloon
into a jump suit.
Left it slumped
on the bathroom floor.

Hitched a ride on a rig
rolling to New York. Climbed
into the rig, the driver said
'Hey, you're…'
'Yeah, The Big Bopper. I faked it,
never died in that 'plane crash.
Keep it under your lid.'
I tapped his hat with my porky fingers.
He nodded. We shared a big secret.

Laid low a while in New York.
Saw my funeral on TV in a midtown bar.
A woman wept on the next stool but one.

'He was everything to me. Everything.
I have a hank of his hair in my bathroom
and one of his shoelaces
taped to my shoulderblade.'

'He was a slob,' I said.
She looked at me like I was poison.
'He was too, too big,' I said.
'He wanted to be small, like
a little fish you might find in a little pond.'

I needed a new identity.
People were looking at me.
A guy on the subway asked me
if I was Richie Valens.

So I jumped a tramp steamer
heading for England.
Worked my passage as a cook.
In storms the eggs
slid off the skillet.

Made my way to London.
Saw a guy, big guy, guy with a briefcase.
Followed him down the alley,
put my blade into his gut
and as the blood shot
I became him
like momma used to say
the loaf became Jesus.

I am Elvis Presley.
I am Ted Hughes.

At my poetry readings I sneer and rock my hips.
I stride the moors
in a white satin jump suit,
bloated as the full moon.

Bless my soul,
what's wrong with me?

At night I sit in my room
and I write, and the great bulbous me
slaps a huge shadow on the wall.

I am writing a poem
about the death of the Queen Mother
but it won't come right.

I look up. Outside a fox peers at me.
I sing softly to it,
strumming my guitar.

Soon, all the foxes
and the jaguars and the pigs
and the crows are gathering
outside my window, peering in.

I sing 'Wooden Heart', 'Blue Hawaii'.
There is the small applause
of paws and feathers.

I am Ted Hughes. I am Elvis Presley.
I am down at the end of a lonely street
and a jump suit rots in a southern coffin
as people pay their respects to a barrage balloon.

I sit here,
I can feel the evening shrinking me
smaller and smaller.
I have almost gone. Ted,
three inches long, perfect.
Elvis, Ted.

Visit

His moustache appears
to be hanging on nothing.

His heart appears to be
on a screen

like a film star
like Gene Kelly

in *Singing in the Rain*.
It appears to me

that Death almost
walked into this room

but if Death came
we would offer him

no orange juice. If
Death came we would

offer him no grapes.
It appears to me

that from this hospital window
you can see Barnsley

laid out like a stroke victim.
A stroke victim

dressed for a wedding
else a funeral.

Visiting time: you could
fry an egg on this clock,

it's so hot.
Yes, nurse, we're

going now. See you,
moustache. Get well

soon. The car park.
See, there is Death

stretching his stinking balaclava
tight over the town

like having a fat pig
sit on your face

like waking up
with the face of a dead pig

your moustache
hanging on nothing.

Early Train, Rain, Wombwell Station

'You could sell me the door.
I need the whole wall,
but I can make do with the door.'

The facts are in the title, you men.
As many facts as we need for now, thank you

very much. You men: regard me
with your feet, as those
are the parts of your bodies
which I am to kiss, and wash.

I am built, said the man
who was talking in the ranks,
to be whispered.
                    Like a secret!
I shout, pleased with my joke.

Are you not tired yet
of calling me 'you men'
she asked, holding me up
as though I was a hanged man.

By the neck, the train
glinted like an eye, and
the guard laughed, the
the driver laughed, the man with
the paper back laughed:

whispered like a secret!
whispered like, as he said,

a secret!

Poem Occasioned by the High Incidence of Suicide amongst the Unemployed

Now then, fatha, how's your Fred?
They found him in the kitchen
with a bullet in his head.

Now then, fatha, how's your John?
They found him in the river
with his donkey jacket on.

Now then, fatha, how's your Bill?
He jumped under a bus
on Spital Hill.

Now then, fatha, how's your Tom?
He blew hissen to pieces
with a home made bomb.

Now then, fatha, how's your Pete?
He's hanging off a lamp post
on Market Street.

Now then, fatha, how's your Rex?
He strangled hissen
wi' his wedding kex.

Now then, fatha, how's your Stan?
He brayed hissen to death
wi' a watterin can.

Now then, fatha, wheers the wives?
They're cutting their sens
wi' carving knives.

Song for Roof Building (Collected in South Yorkshire Light Industry Park, Barnsley)

(To be accompanied by traditional hammering with roof-building tools)

Say a man has three shillings.
Would you tell me, would you tell me
who the man is with the three shillings?

Build part of the roof!

I know he is not me.
It is not me with the three shillings.
Not me with the three bob.

Build part of the roof!

I have seen them, the men
without three shillings
in this land with no poverty.

Build part of the roof!

I have seen them rubbing
their legs together
to keep warm, to make light.

Build part of the roof!

But this is only a song after all
to help me build this roof.
I do not care about the three shillings.

Build part of the roof!

Say a man has three shillings.
Would you tell me, would you tell me
who the man is with the three shillings?

Build part of the roof!

The Force of his Storm Knocked Me from my Stool

Please for this poem assume
that the word tired equals the word fat.

I went to see the doctor about feeling tired
all the time. Waking up tired. Falling
asleep holding a child's Barbie Horse.
Snoring through a guitar being painted.

The doctor advises me to squat on water.
'Feel it soak into your kex' he says. But
I don't wear kex I wear skirts and tops.
On fine days I wear skirts and tops and but and no hat.

Sometimes in a poem you have to put words in to make
t' rhythm. Sometimes you put in silly words to
make the rhyme. Like that word 'water'.

At home, the doctor moans he says he says
I feel so tired, so tired all the time.
His wife says Eat less you tired slobber.

For slobber read doctor, if you would.

At home, I squat in a wet dish.
The water soaks into my skirt. I'm still tired.

Hi, my name is Tony.
Did you know
that the inhabitants of my head
have fifty-two different words
for the word you know as 'tired'?

I hate it when Tony comes into a poem.
I have a capacity for hate.

Hi Tony. Come and sit here.
By the fire.

Moon River: Lives of the Great Comedians

Big Billy Death swigs a beer
of pint. Hey. Wordplay.
Get it?

Georgie Death eats a banana skin.
Visual humour. Get it?

Fanny Death does impressions.
Look! She's a chair! Look!
She's a table! Look!
She's gone! Get it?

Simon Death and the Death Boys.
Vocal harmony. Moon
River.
Get it?

Here come the memoirs
out of the traps like
(get it?) sauce from a bottle:

'I remember the time I played.
Now where was it. There in the middle
of the stage. A moon
suspended over a river. Audience had
no heads, just hats. Satire, I suppose.
Get it?'

'I remember the time. Stoke. Green
sky. Pottery, I suppose. Green sky,
though: green sky.

Pathos: geddit?'

'I recall a show in. Now where.
Waves lapped against something.
I am old and confused. I shall
leave you with a dance. Maestro.
Character humour. Get.'

Big Billy Death signs his face
on the bar. Georgie Death becomes
demented, eats the same banana
twice. Look! Fanny Death is
World War One.
Time for the song, boys, now.
Moon River, dying on its feet.

Henry's Skeleton, George's Leg

Every year they come
for the Head Teacher's conference:
Henry with his skeleton, George with his leg.

This used to be the big house, all the big windows
facing away from the pit, down the formal gardens.
Now they use it for courses, the Authority.
This year, George has put his leg
into a purple tracksuit bottom. Last year
it was a fishnet stocking. Every year
Henry sits the skeleton next to him at dinner.

It stares ahead as they discuss the National Curriculum.

I clear away the plates.
Last night
Henry took his skeleton out
and sat it on a bench in the grounds; an ambulance
screamed along the motorway. George's leg hung from a window.
I went home. I live in the village. My husband

wanted us to make love but I said No.
Not even if I wear my boots? he said.
No, I said, not even if you wear your boots.

My husband works in a sportswear factory.
Anything since the pit shut, he says.

Tonight I will wear a single fishnet stocking
and I will ask him to wear his purple tracksuit,
just the bottoms. He stole the tracksuit from work
under his coat with NCB on the back.

I can feel my bones under my skin.
My husband will not wear his tracksuit. In London
men in suits slam doors shut and put files
back in cabinets. Lights go out. Schools close.

George sleeps with his leg.
Henry hugs his skeleton close. So close.

My husband tugs on his boots and I look over the motorway
to where the pit used to be. I try to shield my breasts
from the noise of the boots.

My nipples will soon be very sore.

Jesus Died from Eating Curtains

My daughter said that
to me the other day.
As she said it my watch
stopped, and my wife
asked me what I was doing
a week on Sunday.

Synchronicity, I suppose
Jung would have called
it. My wife turned back
to the *Observer*, and
I wound my watch up.
For no reason at all

my daughter began to weep,
so I turned her cassette on
and I heard Postman Pat
say to Jess 'Jesus died
from eating curtains.' Okay
I didn't hear that. But

I am concerned about the
state of Poetry, hear?
I'm concerned about its
lack of ambition, about how
you don't often see the word
galoot or the word galosh

in poems. I'm concerned
about the shape of poems,
and I'm concerned that
poems often sound like
poems. Oh, galoot
galosh, galosh, galoot.

Stone, I Presume

second stanza.' That's what he said,
leaning over me in the classroom,
puffing on his tweed pipe, the air

thick with twist and reek. 'Always
start your poems with the second
stanza, my boy, and you won't go far

wrong.' I pondered this in my rooms
in the University. I knew, just knew,
it was the Thirties. 'The Thirties

are a sort of second stanza, aren't
they?' I said to him. The air was
thick with twist and reek. 'I mean

if you take the War poets as a sort
of first stanza, maybe count the
Twenties as the bit of white space

you find between stanzas…' I was
developing a point, nicely. He looked
at me with eyes like carpet tiles.

'If Christ had only had a second
stanza,' he said, the air thick,
'he would only have risen again,

not died at all.' It was a famous
point. I remembered it all through
the war, the period of Austerity,

until the sixties, when my son
came home smoking Pot. I tried to
explain about the second stanza

but he said 'These are the Sixties,
daddy-o. These are today and now.
These days we leave out the

Point of Transit

fire door keep shut
fire door keep shut

It is a long way back
from the First World War
to here
standing with the young people
and their suitcases.

fire door keep shut

I converted all the cinemas
to sound, you know. All
the cinemas around here.
Now it's all noise.
Skiing. That's
all downhill isn't it?
All downhill into something white?

fire door keep shut

In 1915 I looked up
and saw a young boy
struggling through the mud
with his suitcase.
Where are you going? I asked
but it was a silent film
and he answered in subtitles.

fire door keep shut

The words appeared in the mud by his trainers:
I AM GOING SKIING

Skiing? That's all downhill isn't it?
All downhill into something white?

Downhill from the noise
of the trenches
downhill to the white
hair of an old man.

I carry my suitcase across his head.

I carry my suitcase across my head.
I walk across my head
to the fire door. It is shut.

I am on fire.
In subtitles the word FIRE
at my feet fifteen
times as I burn away.

Still Life Life

1   In front of a log fire
in Cumbria a Doctor
from New Zealand

has just said 'I went to
see a 3-D movie once
but I sat in the front row

and I didn't see any of the film because
it all went on behind
my back.'

The word Ha
is issuing from the mouth
of a German girl

who is sitting next to
the Doctor from New Zealand.
It is followed by the word Ha.

2   I went to see a 3-D movie once
but I sat in the front row
and I didn't see any of the film because
it all went on behind my back.

3   The log speaks:

I would rather burn in a fire
than hear this. I would rather
be fashioned into a bookend
than hear this. I would rather
be sawdust than hear this.

The Doctor speaks:

I went to see a 3-D movie once
but I sat in the front row
and I didn't see any of the film because
it all went on behind my back.

Someone writes in a visitors' book:

I enjoyed myself very much. The food
was superb. The company was good. I have
not got enough space to tell you how much
I love staying here.

The shin of a dead man speaks:

Take these chains from my heart
and set me free.

The German girl speaks:

Ha Ha.

Realism (Nothing is Ever Finished)

Whoever said
Night is Black
wasn't kidding.

The children want
wallpaper. You buy them expensive toys
but all they want is wallpaper.

Black wallpaper. Night is really
an empty swimming pool
that you do not realise
is empty so you make
swimming motions in it.

Like this.
Like this.

But you are not wet.

Daddy, I want
a drink of wallpaper.

What kind do you want?
The kind with flowers on?
The kind that looks like a brick wall?

The kind we used to have in kitchens
with blazons of fruit? Bananas?

Any kind
Daddy.

Night is really
a box of spent matches.

No light, you see.

Daddy! More
wallpaper!

Dad, the Donkey's on Fire

There is a burning donkey
at the side of the canal.
It lights up the sky.

Look at the burning donkey.
In Donkey Language it is saying
'Look at me, you bastards,

I am on fire.'
Although it sounds like hee haw.

H e pressed the briefcase and the catches sprang up with a loud
click. Everyone on the bus looked at him. He fished out the
handwritten instructions: 'Get on the 37 at the bus station. The
school is two stops past the Red Lion.' He peered out of the window.
It was foggy. He leaned forward and spoke to the man in front of
him.

'Excuse me, are we anywhere near the Red Lion?'

The man didn't move his head. His cap was old and greasy.

'Are we, er...anywhere near the Red Lion, pal?'

'Don't talk to me about the bastard Red Lion! Just don't talk to
me about the bastard Red Lion, okay?'

The man still hadn't moved. A woman across the aisle said 'Red
Lion? It's here. I'm getting off here.'

As he walked past the man, the man said,

'Don't do it, pal. You may as well leave it in the bloody pot.'

On the pavement the woman said,

'Was it Red Lion or Red Deer?'

'Red Lion.'

'Oh, I am sorry.'

He began to walk the long hill from the Red Deer to the distant
school.

He felt the sweat making his hair prickle as he rang the bell. The
window slid upwards.

'Can I help you?'

'Yes, er, my name's John Dixon. I'm the poet.'

'Yes?'

'er...I'm visiting the school today as...through the Writers-
In-Schools scheme, to talk to the pupils.'

'You're a poet?'

John wondered if she always spoke in questions.

'I try to be.'

She didn't laugh. She turned to the girl who was typing.

'Do you know anything about a poet?'

The girl shook her head.

'Are you sure it's today?'

'The 21st, yes.'

'Yes. What teacher were you meeting?'

'Mr Harrison.'

'Mr Harrison? We don't have a Mr Harrison. We've got a Mrs Harrison. She takes maths. I don't think she'd have much use for a poet, do you?'

'You don't have a Mr Harrison.' It wasn't a question. A bell rang very loudly, drowning out most of her reply. He only caught the last three words.

'...Lord Arthur Morton?'

There was a pause as John Dixon tried to work out a reply. He thought it must be a literary question.

'I'm afraid I'm not familiar with his work.' She didn't smile.

'I said, do you want to be at Lord Arthur Morton? Are you quite sure you want to be at Lord Arthur Morton?'

'I'm sorry, I don't...'

'This is Lord Arthur Morton School. The old grammar. Is it Brookvale you're wanting?'

He seized on the familiar word.

'Brookvale, yes!'

'Just across the road. I should have guessed it would have been Brookvale. They have poets and that kind of thing. I wouldn't have thought they'd have been having one today, though. They once had an arts festival, I believe.'

She pronounced Arts Festival as though it was a crippling disease.

John turned and ran.

A tall man was standing at the school entrance looking worried. John dashed up to him.

'Mr Harrison? John Dixon. Sorry I'm late; my son's been ill.'

He couldn't admit that he'd been to the wrong school. Harrison shook John's hand and began to hurry him down the corridor. Mr Harrison spoke very quickly.

'Did you get the letter? We've had to make a few changes to the schedule.'

'I didn't get a letter.'

'What? Didn't you?' He stopped walking. He looked as though he was going to weep. He thumped the wall.

'Oh, the bloody secretary. The bloody, bloody secretary!'

'It doesn't matter. It'll be okay.' They began to walk again, faster.

'Anyway, if you didn't get the letter, I don't suppose it matters. Nothing bloody matters!' He laughed, extremely loudly.

'So what am I doing first?'

'First you're reading to the first year, then you'll be doing a workshop with the second year, then after lunch it's two workshops with the third year.'

This time it was John's turn to stop. He had gone cold.

'First years? I don't usually work with first years.'

'Oh, you'll be okay. Thick as planks the lot of them. They really are a dumb bloody year.'

'I suppose...'

'They don't know anything about you. There hasn't been time. They're sitting in a drama studio so I suppose the thick sods think they're getting a play.'

'Can you introduce me?'

'Can't you just get on with it?'

'It's nice to be introduced. It gets it off to a good start.'

'Okay then, if you like.' They approached a door. From behind it John could hear the sound of slow, rhythmic handclapping. They walked into the room. There was a quick, empty silence, and then the room exploded into laughter. Someone shouted 'I fancy him!' and someone else said 'He looks a right wally!' John scuttled to the corner of the room like an insect. He looked at the rows of children. They looked huge. They looked to be in their early thirties. First years. What the hell do you say to first years? He was used to working with sixth formers; polite and shy or volatile and dismissive but always in some kind of relationship to his status as a famous poet. Harrison was yelling at the rows of laughing faces.

'Right. I'm waiting. Thank you. Thank you...'

The noise gradually subsided. The room became terribly quiet. John opened his briefcase and the catches sprang up with a loud crack. Mr Harrison spoke, too loudly for the echoing room:

'Right. We've got this poet on now. He's turned up. Poets are supposed to be late, anyway. I don't know much about him. Here he is.'

John walked across the floor to the table in the complete angry silence. Someone whispered, loud enough for him to hear, 'He looks a boring bastard.' He opened his mouth, cleared his throat.

'Thank you Mr Harrison, er...'

The laughter bellowed at him again.

John and the man who wasn't Mr Harrison walked into the staffroom. People began to speak to each other in indecipherable code.

'Got the eighteens?' said a very old man in a track suit. The man who wasn't Mr Harrison nodded.

'They're over in K7. I brought the Hunstanton, too.'

John stood on his own.

'Sorry I thought you were Mr Harrison,' he said to the smoky air near the man's back.

'He thought I was Harrison!'

'Christ!' the man in the tracksuit laughed.

'What is your name?' asked John.

'er...Frank Smith.'

'Bloody Hell!' The man in the tracksuit seemed shocked. Frank Smith said 'I'm not sure who you're with next. Sorry that last lot weren't too keen. Ignorant little sods. Mind you, I think you were a bit over their heads. Sorry they got a bit restless.'

'I thought they might have asked a few more questions.'

'Yes. Would you like a cup of coffee?'

'Yes please. Black. No sugar.'

'Sorry, they only do white. Out of a big bloody teapot. Look, would you look after yourself for a bit. I've got to see somebody. Harry could...' He looked around but the man in the tracksuit had gone.

'Anyway, you'll be okay. After break, either me or somebody else will be down to get you for the workshop. Actually it probably won't be me, but somebody'll come...' he backed out of the door as he spoke. The bell rang. Everyone in the staffroom moaned. A man turned to John and said,

---

'Always the same, you just get to the bloody coffee…'

'I've got Darren Southwell next,' said a small dark-haired woman, 'pray for me.'

They all laughed. John laughed. The first man spoke again.

'Darren Southwell? No, you're okay. Moira's put him down for that creative writing workshop. Some poor poet coming along to try and drill some culture into us. Poor bugger.'

'Bloody hell! Darren'll eat him alive!'

'Mind you, have you heard how much he's getting? Forty quid!'

'Hey, we're in the wrong game here! What's that line again… I wandered lonely as a…what?'

'Pillock?'

They all laughed. John didn't laugh. He'd asked for £50. The dark haired woman spoke again.

'I wouldn't have thought they'd have had a poet today, what with…'

'Oh, sod that!'

'So to speak!' They all laughed again. The woman turned to John.

'Are you here for the interview?'

'Yes,' John lied.

'Don't come and work in this place, it's a madhouse.'

'And a dump.'

'Mind you, there'll be a few more vacancies soon; we're all going to be poets.' They laughed again, then moved quickly out of the room. The staffroom was now empty except for a woman collecting coffee cups, three young men in suits, and John. The men in suits were obvious interviewees.

John glanced at his watch. 11:05. The lesson ended at five past twelve. With a bit of luck he wouldn't have to do too much. He sat down and began to leaf through the *Times Educational Supplement*.

At 11:15 he began to worry, began to feel guilty. For £50, even for £40, he ought to be working. One of the interviewees leaned over and said 'You should have worn a suit, you know, mate. They don't go much on casual dress here. Some places you could get away with it, but not at this place.'

John was trying to think of a reply when a tall, nervous man ran in. He began to shout in a theatrical voice.

'Why isn't that stupid man with 2C? The wretched poet! He seems to have sloped off somewhere…'

Sloped off. Wretched. John noted the anachronisms,

'I'm the poet,' he said. 'I was told to wait here and somebody would fetch me.'

'Who told you that? That's not what I said! Who told you?'

'Frank Smith.'

The tall man swayed as though he had been hit. He put his hand to his mouth in a swift gesture, then turned and ran from the room. John didn't know what to do, what he had said to offend the man. He stood for a second and then walked out after him. He had the impression that the man had gone right. He turned right and walked briskly down the corridor. He glanced at his watch. 11:23. He'd soon have no time left to write any poetry with them. He realised he didn't really know what he was looking for. He turned to a boy who had suddenly appeared beside him.

'Excuse me. Do you know where I might find the second year?'

'Which second year?'

'How do you mean?'

'I mean what form does it reckon to be?'

'I'm not sure.'

'I should try the office. If there's anybody there. They're probably all at the funeral.'

'Another poet?'

'What?'

'It doesn't matter. Thanks. Where *is* the office, by the way?'

'Down there, on the left.'

John walked into the office. The tall man was sitting at a desk. He was clutching a cup of coffee. His eyes were red. He looked up at John.

'Are you satisfied?'

'I'm sorry; I don't know what you mean. I'm looking for that second year.'

'Oh, sod the bloody second year!'

A woman came in.

'You shouldn't upset yourself, Mr Harrison. Look, I think it would be best if you went home.'

'I don't want to go home. I want to carry on as if nothing. Had. Happened.' He spoke the last three words very slowly.

'Perhaps you ought to have gone to the funeral . . . you really should have . . .'

'No. It had to end there. With him.'

John felt like an intruder.

'Is it Frank Smith who's dead? And are you Mr Harrison?'

The telephone rang. Nobody answered it. The tall man smiled.

'I should be more hospitable, Mr Dixon. I'm normally here to welcome my poets . . .'

He put both hands to his face. He began to sob. He rubbed his eyes savagely.

'I think it's best if you go now, Mr Dixon. Really, I do,' the woman said.

'No. No. He should stay,' said Mr Harrison.

'I think it is best if you go,' said the woman.

The Route to Work

They were discussing it again when he got in the car. Paul jerked the car away from the kerb, almost, David thought, as though he was jerking a dog away from something interesting in a patch of grass.

'She's a very stubborn girl,' said Paul, glancing at the rearview mirror. David closed his eyes and thought about the day ahead. John smiled and tried, really tried, to make a joke. Paul ignored it.

'Our final authority has to be Jesus Christ in matters like this,' he said. He said *Jesus Christ* in an undertone, like he was swearing.

'But if you look at the reason St Paul says it...' said John.

'The reason St Paul says it,' said Paul as though he was about to bellow. He didn't bellow. He went quiet. He spoke again, quietly.

'The reason is that the women in the early church...' John interrupted him.

'Yes, in the early church they were so excited about their new found freedom in Christ. They jumped around and made a lot of noise, and that's why St Paul says they should wait until later to ask. Ask questions at home.'

Outside, an old postman struggled with a bulging sack.

They drove up the hill past Wombwell station. The sky was a slab of red in the earlyish morning light. John tried again to make a joke but Paul was determined to keep the mood serious.

'I ought to tell my wife about that obey bit,' said David. He felt suddenly uncomfortable. He put his hand in his jacket pocket and pulled out a tomato. He felt embarrassed. He also felt a little sad. He opened his carrier bag and dropped the tomato in.

'In 1662 women were chattels,' said Paul, his face reddening. 'I tell you this, it was all I could do to keep my temper...'

It seemed to David that Paul was saying things in the wrong order, out of sequence. He wasn't making a lot of sense.

'They did everything the man asked them to. When they married the man took all their goods as though they were his own.'

They slowed down at the traffic lights on Platts Common. On the left a fat man in a vivid red track suit pounded along the pavement. On the right a woman carried a box of vegetables into a shop from a van.

'Things have changed today…' The lights changed. They moved. Paul continued to speak. The words seemed clearer now.

'He ought to understand the relationship between a man and a woman, that the relationship has changed…'

David felt in his pocket again. Another tomato, big and ripe. Not a good salad one but okay for frying. He dropped it in the carrier bag. There was a pause. John spoke.

'So, what's the next step going to be?'

David thought about the journey to work and the idea of the Journey to Work. The idea of the sacredness, holiness of the Journey. It seemed silly to point out to himself that if you worked in the same place for a long time you never varied your route to work. Or the mode of transport. Instead of car every day, this route every day, it could be car one day, bike the next, some days roller skates. Some days a giant airship disfiguring the sky over Grenoside.

'Well, they're coming down this weekend. They're going to see him.' Paul appeared to be changing more gears than there were in the car. The car had slowed to a halt in traffic and David was able to look into the house on his left. There were four tomatoes ripening on the windowsill. An old man slumped in an armchair, asleep in front of breakfast television.

'But I tell you this, she can be a very stubborn girl.'

Two more tomatoes, one in each pocket. One seemed to be striped, but it couldn't be. No, it wasn't. He checked again. Yes, it was.

Yes, it was.

'They don't understand the changing relationship between men and women.'

They slowed down. Debbie was waiting. She climbed into the car. It was the first time they had seen each other for three days. They all said Hello. It was like a poem consisting of only the word Hello and no other words, or a list containing only the word Hello.

'I hated the whole thing. I'm absolutely knackered,' said Debbie.

'That's a shame. You were looking forward,' said John.

'The weather must have been appalling,' said Paul.

'The hailstones were hurting our faces, one bit…'

'We're still in the middle of the Obey Debate here,' said John.

'She shouldn't bother with it at all…'

The sky was getting redder. Do I understand that? Do you understand any of this? Do I understand that at this point, or around this point, the story changes? It changes.

We are in the mind of the man in the house. The old man, slumped, asleep. The television is watching him. David is talking to the man and it is as though he is interviewing him. The man is speaking in his head. David is speaking in his head.

'I remember before the war when all this was tomatoes. Before even this road had been thought of, before the man who painted the white lines on the road had even been born. Tomatoes, all of it. And then the planners came. And they decided to knock down all those lovely rows of terraced tomatoes and throw up those high rise tomatoes in their place. And the tomato always breaks down. You have to climb the tomatoes. And that's no good if you're my age.'

'What do you remember about the war?'

'In a crater, up to my waist in mud. Tomatoes bursting overhead. My mate lying beside me, dead as a tomato. Then a bullet got me, right in the chest. And I thought "I'm a goner. My tomato's up." But there wasn't any blood. I felt in my pocket and do you know what? My grandfather's old tomato had saved me. The bullet was lodged in it. That tomato he brought in 1867 from Wales, and gave me on my fourteenth birthday when he was too old to hold a fork. It was a miracle.'

'What can you tell me about love?'

'Not much. This. My old wife. When she was my young wife, standing there naked and superb on our wedding night. She held a tomato in her hand and I sat on a stool drawing her on clean white paper. So as not to forget it. Her there, naked and superb, and me concentrating on the tomato, drawing it with great care. What you might call infinite care.'

'And what can you tell me about Death?'

'My old mum used to say "Open any cupboard and you'll find it" and she meant Death. When Len died who should be the one to break down at the grave but Betty. "I loved him more than I loved my…"'

'Tomatoes?'

'No.'

You must agree that to go back to the car now would be a betrayal. To return to that debate on whether Paul's daughter should agree to obey her husband would be a slap in the face for this story. We cannot stay with the old man either. He has discarded the tomato motif. The emblem that I've been trying to carve into the story like a mark in a piece of silver has gone. We can go nowhere. To end, though, to tie the story up, I will walk over to Len's funeral in the pouring rain.

It was raining. The kind of rain that loves funerals. I broke through the hedge and began to walk briskly towards the little gang of people at the graveside. I was in my shirtsleeves and I was soaked. They were just lowering the coffin in. Betty was crying. A strong man had his arm around her shoulders. Betty began to speak.

'I loved him. I loved him more than I loved my…'

It is right that her words are lost in a crash of sobbing from the strong man. I lean over towards Betty's mouth, placing my ear against it like you would place a limpet shell over the mouth of a plastic bottle. I hear nothing. She loved him. Perhaps that is enough.

Whatever Happened to Freddie Galloway?

It was 1962, and I was in Mrs Hudson's class at Low Valley Juniors; it was Monday morning, it was raining and it was the day the school photographer came. My mam stood there with the rainmate in her hand, and I stood there sobbing.

'I'll look daft in a rainmate,' I said, my breath coming in great heaving gulps; 'I'll look like a lass.' My mam wasn't impressed.

'You'll not look like a lass! How can you look like a lass with knees like that?' She arranged my hair one last time and then placed the rainmate carefully over it.

'You are not going to look like Alfalfa for your school photo; you are not going to sit on Auntie Mabel's mantelpiece like a scarecrow!'

All the relatives got my school photo for an additional Christmas present; me smiling out on front rooms from the Borders of Scotland to the North Derbyshire coalfield. I had the kind of hair that stuck up like a brush, so on the weekend before the photos I always had to go to Mad Geoff's for my hair cut. I never fathomed why they called him Mad Geoff, except that he always wore a dicky bow which I suppose sets you apart in a village like ours.

I'd gone after school on the Friday night; Mad Geoff was empty except for Bing, sitting there in his trilby and serenading us with 'Three Coins in The Fountain'. When we came in Bing stopped singing and, looking at my mother, said to Geoff, 'Has tha gow owt for't weekend?' and Geoff said, 'Aye, a country cottage.' My mam stared into space.

When I got into the chair Geoff said, 'What does tha want then, Richard? Tony Curtis? Dickie Valentine? Fabian? Elvis?' I was about to say Fabian when my mother said 'He wants a light trim. A very light trim.' Bing repeated the order: 'He wants a light trim, Mad. An extremely light trim.' Geoff was famous for his enthusiastic cutting, and anything other than a light trim came out like what my dad called a barrack room special.

As Geoff trimmed and his clippers buzzed I heard Bing telling my mam about The Daz Man.

'They reckon they'll be coming round this area next week, Mrs M., so you'd better keep your eye open for 'em.'

'They'll not be coming round here,' said my mam scornfully. 'The rent man's the only one that comes round here.'

'Well, you'd better have your packet of Daz ready, Missus,' Bing piped up, 'if you complete that slogan they'll give you a ten bob note.'

Geoff just missed my ear with his clippers. 'Aye, and if you believe that you'll stand for't egg under't cap,' and then whipped the sheet off me and said, 'Does that want any jollop on it?' I was about to say yes when my mam said, 'He does not! It took two days to wash it out last time!'

'Who's the Daz Men, mam?' I asked as we walked home through the park.

'It's just some daft stuff off the telly. Some soft articles who come knocking on your door because they've got nowt better to do.'

Now it was Monday morning and I was walking to school in the rain with a rainmate on. I tried to hide behind my mam as we caught up with Robert Doughty. If he saw me in a rainmate he'd never let me forget it. As we drew level with Mrs Doughty and Robert my mam turned to me in triumph.

'There, Richard. I told you it was a good idea.'

There was Robert Doughty, the cock of class six, with a rainmate on. A pink rainmate. He looked at me with murder in his eyes.

In the cloakroom my mam took the rainmate off and folded it up. She patted my hair nervously.

'What time's the photographer coming, anyway?' she asked.

'Two o'clock, Mrs Matthewman,' said Robert, still with his rainmate on. He looked like a sea anemone.

'Two o'clock?' said my mam in horror. 'How are you going to keep your hair tidy till two o'clock?'

'I'll make sure Richard keeps his rainmate on,' said Robert, angelically.

Assembly was taken by Miss Parkin. We sang 'When a Knight won his Spurs', said some prayers and then Miss Parkin looked at us and said, 'Well, I can see you've all remembered that the school photographer is coming today. And this year we're going to try something a little bit different. As well as the individual photos, we're going to do some class photographs. That means in years to come, when you're all big boys and girls, you'll be able to look at the pictures with fond memories. Now, who knows what fond memories are?' A forest of hands shot up, mainly from the youngest infants. Miss Parkin pointed to Mary Till, who was straining her arm upwards and snapping her fingers enthusiastically.

'Yes, Mary. What are Fond Memories?'

Mary looked doubtful.

'Fond Memories, Mary. Do you know what we mean when we say Fond Memories?'

'Seven,' said Mary.

'That's nearly right Mary. Have another go. Fond Memories.'

'Seventy ten,' said Mary, triumphantly. Miss Parkin signalled to Mrs Hinchcliffe to begin the music, and we filed out to Ravel's *Bolero*.

Everybody was excited about the photographer coming; we'd all come in our best clothes, and at least five lads in our class had been brought to school with rainmates on. Mrs Hudson said that we all looked a picture already and Noel Ramsden said we looked like Fond Memories and Mrs Hudson smiled and gave him a star.

At playtime Mrs Hudson warned us: no running about, no fighting, no donkey rides, no football. Robert Doughty came up.

'Where's your rainmate, Richard? I promised your mam you'd wear it.'

I tried to ignore him. The rainmate was in my pocket. Robert walked right up to me, pressing himself against me.

'I said where's your rainmate. You've got to wear your rainmate or your dad'll get his belt out. I heard your mam tell my mam. Get your rainmate on.'

I felt the tears welling up in my eyes.

'It's not raining,' I said, quietly.

'Put it on anyway, or I'll squeeze your balloons.'

I didn't know what that meant but it sounded painful. I got the rainmate out and put it on. Everybody laughed. The tears splashed down my cheeks. Mrs Robinson came out and rang the bell, and we all lined up. Everybody was looking at me. Mrs Robinson said,

'You can take your rainmate off now Richard, but that's a very sensible boy for putting it on.'

I wiped my eyes with my cuff and allowed myself a little smile.

We'd just started back after play when a big boy came round with a note. Mrs Hudson read it and said, 'Will you all please stop what you're doing, please. Now.' We all sat quietly and looked at Mrs Hudson. She had bright red lips which were famous throughout the school. In those days most teachers didn't wear lipstick and if they did it was something pale and subtle. Not Mrs Hudson: she lit the classroom up like a beacon as she welcomed us each morning. And now those bright red lips were pursed like she didn't understand the message that the big boy had brought.

'This note has just come round from Miss Parkin, and it's very serious so I want you all to pay attention.' She read it carefully. 'There are some people in the village with a doz hats but you are on no account to take one of them if offered.' Mrs Hudson put the note down and looked at us. 'Doz. That's a dozen.'

She looked at me.

'How many hats is a dozen, Richard?'

'Daz hats,' I said. I felt like Mary Till.

'Yes, all right. How many is a doz.'

'They Daz hats, Mrs Hudson,' said Freddie Galloway.

'I know there's a doz, Freddie, but how *many* is that?' I could see that Mrs Hudson was getting exasperated. She'd moved from the Forest of Dean when her husband's pit shut and sometimes she couldn't understand a word we said.

'It's Daz like off the telly, Miss,' said Freddie. 'Blokes are coming round and if you get words reight they gi thi a big hat. It's only for a laugh.'

Mrs Hudson looked more puzzled than ever. She folded the note up and put it on her desk.

'Anyway, Class Six; these people need their hats. You are not to take one. Now get on with your poems about "My Favourite Feeling".'

Dinnertime came round quickly. I gobbled my dinner down and went out to play; the weather was still dismal, and the supply teacher from Huddersfield was bundled up in scarves and a big fawn duffel coat. We called him Green Un because he looked just like the man from the Sue Ryder Home who sold the Green Un outside Harry and Jud's shop on a Saturday afternoon. I wandered up to the gate, and looked out. The pit bus went past taking the afternoon shift, and I waved to my dad. He didn't wave back, just sat there staring into space.

Behind the pit bus there was a brightly coloured van that looked just like a packet of soap powder, driven by a man in a white trilby. It was the Daz Hats! The van stopped outside the gates and the man got out. Word spread instantly and loads of us crowded round the gate.

'Who'd like a hat? Anybody like a hat?'

We were hesitant at first, then Noel Ramsden said, 'I'll have one!' The man put his hand into a bag and pulled out a big blue hat with WASHES WHITER on it. Noel put it on and we all laughed. Noel said, 'I don't know the slogan' and the man said, 'It doesn't matter, kid. It doesn't matter. Let's just get rid of some of these bloody hats!'

We all recoiled a bit at the rude word, but then surged forward when he started to pull the hats out of the bag. I got one: it was too big and it flopped over my ears but it didn't seem to matter. We were all running about and laughing. Bill Lillee had two hats on, and Robert Doughty was throwing his up in the air and catching it.

Suddenly we all went quiet. Miss Parkin was standing there, her face pale with fury.

'Just what do you think you are doing Keith Barlow?' she said to the man with the hats. He looked sheepish.

'Just giving out these hats like for a joke Miss Parkin.'

'You've been in the George by the state of you, as well. You've not changed since I used to teach you, Keith Barlow, you've not changed a bit. Now get away and take those silly hats with you.'

He climbed into the van and drove off. We were very impressed by the fact that Miss Parkin seemed to know everybody in the world. She turned her anger on us: 'I'm surprised at you, I really am. Now give me those ridiculous hats and you can go back to your classrooms because the photographer will be here in a minute. Fond memories, children, remember? Fond memories.'

I passed her my hat but I was surprised to see that some people were taking a huge risk by stuffing theirs into their pockets or down their jumpers. One fell on the floor and Miss Parkin picked it up with a smile. We filed into the classroom.

Mrs Hudson licked her finger and smoothed my hair down as

we queued up to go to the photographer. She smiled at me, and I smiled back. The photographer had a little horse puppet and he shouted, 'Watch the Horsey!' to make us look happy on the picture. After all the individual ones were done, we had to group together for the class photo. The little ones sat at the front, and I stood at the back with the other big lads. I had Robert Doughty on one side, and Freddie Galloway on the other.

Once the photographer had us all settled he waggled the horse puppet and shouted, 'Watch the Horsey!' and at that moment lots of things happened at once.

Freddie Galloway pulled a Daz hat out of his pocket and put it on and at the same time Robert Doughty fished one out of his cardigan and jammed it on my head. Miss Parkin ran across the room like she was being chased and the camera flashed. I'll always remember that moment, and what it led to: Robert and Freddie being sent home, and the start of Freddie's long decline that ended in 1991 when the pit shut and he took to wandering between the George, the Sportsman and the Drop through the long afternoons.

When Miss Parkin died, her sister came to see me. I'd just started teaching and I was doing some work at the kitchen table. She came in and said, 'Miss Parkin wanted you to have this; she always knew you'd amount to something.'

It was the picture. Me with the hat crushed on my head, Robert Doughty looking wicked, and Freddie Galloway smiling innocently beneath his big blue brim. Washes Whiter. Fond Memories.

Grisp the Wheel at Ten Past Two

The car horn hooted outside. I didn't move. I stood looking at myself in the mirror. The spot on my neck was huge. Vesuvius, the kids at school called it. I'd been teaching there two terms. The longest two terms of my life. September 1977 to April 1978. At least thirty years to go. Then, sitting on the bus on the way home the other night, a gang of big women from the tennis-ball factory got on. They always got on at that time. They smelled of rubber and scent, and they took over the bus. One sat next to me. She stared at my neck. I felt myself getting red. The woman in front was showing the woman next to her photos of the Queen Mother's recent visit to Barnsley. 'That's her hand, waving,' she was saying. 'Eee, hasn't she got lovely gloves on!' I tried to lean over to see the pictures and the woman next to me said, 'What's that on your neck?'

The two women in front turned round slowly. My neck was more interesting than the Queen Mother's gloves, waving. I stood up and got off the bus, a mile before the house.

The horn hooted again. I went outside. The driving instructor's car was white, and not as new as it could have been. 'Don's Driving School,' it said on top. Don himself sat inside; he was a small, balding man, and I noticed that he was wearing the biggest pair of sandals I'd ever seen. He looked at me, then looked at my neck, and sucked in his breath.

'I don't get many your age,' he said. 'It's mainly kids, just past their seventeenth birthday. It's mainly kids.'

All my mates in the lower sixth had got driving lessons for their seventeenth birthday. Dave Sunderland had got a car. It sat in the drive as he took lesson after lesson and failed test after test. He washed it every Sunday and always sent for AA road maps for his holiday with his mam, and then sat studying them on the coach as the car gathered rust and a cat had kittens underneath it. Eventually he passed and drove to the shop in triumph for his mother's regular order of Advocaat. And that left only me. I once asked a girl out in that summer after I left school and before I went to college. I said I'd meet her at the bus stop opposite the cemetery. She looked at me with withering contempt and said 'You can't be a man with a ticket in your hand.' Her parents got the *Manchester Guardian* and she was going to Art College in Falmouth.

Don shifted his sandals and looked at me again and said, 'Not many your age like I say, not many your age.'

'Well, I'm fed up of the bus,' I said. 'Slow, overcrowded, and I've to wait in the bus station for another one. Two buses to catch, an hour and forty minutes door-to-door and it's only eight miles.'

'I bet kids on the bus take the michael out of that thing on your neck and all,' he said. 'I bet kids on the bus take the michael.' He drove us to a layby just outside the village. We changed places. As I got out I noticed that his sandals flapped like flippers.

'Right. Comfortable?'

'Er…yes.'

'OK. This is the brake. This is the clutch. This is the accelerator.'

My neck was killing me; a heavy, continual pain that made it hard to grasp what he was saying.

'I said, turn it on. Use the key. Turn it on using the key.'

I almost said, no, I've changed my mind, got out and walked away. I didn't really want to learn to drive. I enjoyed being in cars, enjoyed being a passenger, but being a driver, in charge of a lethal machine that could kill and maim, no thanks. But I thought about the bus station in February and the factory women and the bloke with the stick who always saw me on the bus and made a point of sitting next to me and showing me the scars on his back, and I turned the engine on and tried to proceed into the traffic, as I'd seen my dad do many many times.

The car leaped forward like a kangaroo and there was a terrible crashing of gears. Don grabbed the wheel from me and a huge articulated lorry went past, blaring its horn.

Don was white and sweating. I thought driving instructors were meant to be calm.

'Bloody Hell Fire, I mean Bloody Hell Fire! What were you trying to do? Kill us both? We'd have ended up looking like that thing on your neck if that artic had flattened us. We'd have looked like that thing on your neck if that artic had flattened us. That thing on your neck.' I noticed that when Don got agitated he repeated things even more.

Somehow we got into the stream of traffic and crawled down the road. Don was a bit calmer, although a twitch had started ticking away under his left eye. I hunched over the wheel like a cop in Highway Patrol.

'Relax,' said Don. 'Relax. Relax.' I tried to relax.

'You're not holding the wheel properly. You're not holding it properly. You've got to grisp the wheel at ten past two.'

'Don't you mean grip the wheel at ten to two?'

Don's twitch went into top gear. 'Grisp it, grisp it. Grisp the wheel at ten past two. Grisp the wheel at ten past two!' I grisped it, both hands round the right side of the wheel, and he slapped my hand.

'Like this, like this!' he said, holding his hands up in the ten-to-two position. We drove on. I stalled at traffic lights, drove in first gear. I felt my collar chafing at my neck. The hour was almost over. 'Turn left up this hill,' said Don. 'Turn left up this hill. Turn left up this hill.' I turned left. Snape Hill, very steep indeed. The car juddered and began to lose power. 'Change gear. Change gear. Change gear. Change gear,' said Don, his twitch dancing madly under his eye. I was in second gear and the hill was too steep. I needed to get into first. I changed gear. Into fourth. The gearbox almost exploded and the gearstick leaped out of my hand. The car stopped. A bread van almost crashed into us, and then swerved by, the driver gesturing madly. Don gestured back, theatrically, giving a deliberate two finger salute with the fingers spread very wide and the hand going up and down very slowly. It made me think of the Queen Mother's gloved hand and I had to stifle a giggle. I coughed.

'It's not funny. It's not funny. This car is my living. My living.'

'I'm sorry.'

'Well be more careful. Be more bloody careful.'

We got slowly to the top of the hill. Don wiped his face with a big hanky. 'Slow down here. Pull in here.'

'What for?'

'Just slow down here. Pull in here. Pull in here.'

The car ground to a halt outside the Methodist chapel. On the notice board there was a poster which read 'Well Done is Better Than Well Said'.

'I won't be a minute,' said Don, clambering out of the car, sandals flapping. I wound the window down and leaned out.

'Why, where are you going?'

'I've got to get some sticks,' he said. At least that's what I think he said. He went round the back of the chapel. I sat there in the pale sun and felt the thing on my neck. It hurt. It was sort of soft round the bottom and then hard round the top. Like a nipple.

After a while I noticed a woman looking at me through the open window. It was the woman who'd sat next to me on the bus.

'You want to see a doctor with that,' she said. I tried to look away, as though I'd got something phenomenally interesting in the glove box. Her eyes bored into my neck. 'My uncle had one of them. The doctor had to clean it out with a wire.'

I couldn't stand it anymore. Where the hell was Don? I got out of the car. Where was Don going to get sticks in a chapel?

The side door of the chapel was open, so I went in. The room felt cool and smelt of polish. I could hear a voice muttering at the far end of the big room. It was Don. He was standing in the pulpit reading something, but you could hardly hear him. I walked down the aisle towards him. An old lady in a big blue hat looked at me and smiled. I noticed that someone was lying in one of the pews, asleep. It was Phil Allsop, the Methodist Sunday School leader. As I looked at him, he woke up. I went to school with Phil; he was always a bit holy. He once told Mr Drinkwater that he should take Jesus into his life and Mr Drinkwater clipped him round the head with a hardback copy of *The White Company* by Sir Arthur Conan Doyle. Phil sat up, rubbing his eyes. He looked exhausted. He worked in the offices at the bed factory because his mother used to say he was delicate. I noticed that he deliberately wasn't looking at the thing on my neck.

'All right, Richard. It's good to see you in the house of the Lord. What brings you here?'

'I'm looking for Don. I'm supposed to be having a driving lesson with him.' Phil looked distressed.

'Well, that's just not fair. He told me he'd cleared his diary. We're only up to Numbers as well.'

I was baffled. 'I'm sorry, but I don't know what you're talking about.'

'I did the whole night shift. Bill Ellis was supposed to do the four a.m. section but glory knows where he got to ... I had to do all night on my own and now I don't know if I'm coming or going. And

Don was meant to do three hours this morning and he was almost an hour late. It's just not on!' He sounded close to tears.

'I still don't know what you're on about,' I said.

Phil looked at me as though he was seeing me for the first time. His eyes were almost shutting as he spoke.

'I'm sorry. I'm so tied up in this thing. It's to raise funds for the Sunday School outing. We're having a sponsored neck reading.'

'Pardon?'

'A sponsored bible reading. The whole lot from Genesis to Revelation; should take about four days altogether. We're supposed to do two hour shifts but I've been quite badly let down by my volunteers.'

'You said sponsored neck reading.'

Further down the church in the pulpit Don stopped muttering and shouted, 'I won't be a minute. I'll just get to the end of this chapter. I'll just get to the end of this chapter.' Phil turned to him in despair.

'Oh, Don! Can't you stay another hour? I've got Violet Mullis coming at twelve. Her sister's bringing her from the home.'

'I can't. I can't. I've got to get Stirling Moss here home and then I've got another lesson with him that won the pools. I've got to get Stirling Moss here home and then I've got another lesson with him that won the pools.' He put his head down and carried on muttering, turning a page. Phil sat down heavily; he looked older, somehow. In fact he looked the spitting image of photographs I'd seen of his Grandap Allsop in the trenches. It must have been the quality of light in the chapel. I know one thing: my neck was giving me some hell.

'Don't worry about it, Phil,' I said. 'I'll get the bus home. I don't think me and driving are meant for each other.' I felt in my pocket and gave him some change. More than I intended, actually. 'Here, have this for the Sunday School outing.'

He smiled, and the years seemed to fall away from him. He looked at the money and I remembered that after Mr Drinkwater had hit him with the copy of *The White Company* Phil had smiled and said, 'I forgive you, Mr Drinkwater, you didn't know what you were doing.' So Mr Drinkwater hit him again with Lamb's *Tales from Shakespeare*. Maybe he'd end up a saint. Phil, not Mr Drinkwater.

Phil looked at the money. 'Well, every bit helps,' he said, 'but we've a long way to go before we reach our neck.'

I went outside before I hit him. I knew how Mr Drinkwater felt. The sun had gone in and it was blowing cold. The old lady in the big blue hat followed me out; she reached over and touched me on the arm.

'That thing on your neck,' she said, in a thin, quavering voice, 'my late, dear husband had one in the fifties. Around the time the first sputnik destroyed the weather. I rubbed it with lard every night. That got rid of it. Try it. Try lard. Only the best lard, of course.' She turned and went back into the chapel.

Lard! What a stupid idea. I walked down the street to the bus stop, then turned round and went to the shop on the corner. I looked at the lard, smug in its tight white packets. I caught sight of my reflection in the shop window. The thing on my neck looked as big as a satsuma. I picked up a packet of lard and took it to the till.

'What's that thing on your neck?' the lad behind the counter said, as he put my lard in a carrier.

'Just give me the lard,' I said. 'Just give me the lard. Just give me the lard.'

There's Always a Man in a Cardigan

Lindsay sat up and said, 'I've started.' I sat up in bed and looked at the clock: 0101. It seemed more like a cry for help than a time. 'Are you sure?' I said, tentatively. I remembered the time two days before when I'd come home from school to find her holding on to the occasional table and trying to take her mind off things by watching Tony Hart make a mural out of sugar lumps. We'd dashed through Barnsley faster than the police did during the Ronald Biggs in Mexborough rumour, but when we got to the maternity unit it was a false alarm.

'I'm sure,' she said, 'get the car out, you're going to be a dad.' She came downstairs slowly, deliberately, her face occasionally twisting up with pain. I'd told her I was going to be there at the birth but now I wasn't so sure. I think really I'd have liked to pace about outside and then get called in to see a face in a shawl and start handing out cigars. For years I didn't know that I'd been born. My mam said the nurse had brought me through the snow. I asked why the nurse had to bring me, and my mam said she would have brought me herself but she was in bed poorly at the time. Later, when I was at junior school, Pud Stennett explained how babies were born. It was a rainy Saturday afternoon in 1965 in my auntie's shed and me and Pud had just tried to smoke some balsa wood cigarettes.

'You know breasts,' he said. Breasts. The word made me go red. He said it again. 'You know breasts.' 'Yes.' 'Well you know the bits at the end.'

'What bits?'

'Nittles.'

'Nittles?'

'Nittles. Women feed their babies through 'em. Well, that's how the babies are born. Through the nittles.'

'How do you mean?' The balsa wood smoke was starting to get to me. I felt a bit sick. Pud lowered his voice as though my Auntie might be standing outside the shed, listening.

'Well half the baby's born through one nittle and the other half's born through the other nittle and then the doctor sews you together and that's why you've got a belly button. It's where your halves were put together by a doctor.'

I was overwhelmed. I didn't know what to say. Then a sudden thought occurred to me.

'What about twins?' I asked. Stennett's voice was even softer now.

'I know but I can't tell thi.'

'I'll give thi all my spare civil war cards.'

Pud Stennett loved civil war cards, and I saw he couldn't resist my offer.

He leaned very close to me. His face looked old and wise in the stale balsa wood smoke.

'Four nittles,' he said.

I got the car out of the garage and Lindsay struggled in. It was a clear, crisp moonless night in December, and I could see my breath as I closed the garage door. Funny thing about Pud Stennett. He ended up teaching biology.

The car started first time and we were off. Lindsay sat in the back, me driving slowly, trying not to panic. It was only a few months since I'd passed my test and I still wasn't too confident. Lindsay leaned forward and said, 'You can try second gear if you want,' and I bit back a stinging reply.

My Auntie Elsie always used to say, 'Tell 'em about the jam when the fire's gone out' which apparently meant 'Always try to keep people's mind off things' so I said to Lindsay, 'Would you like some music on the 8-track? I've got Jethro Tull, Fairport Convention.' I was still into progressive in those days. She shook her head.

'Just try and drive a bit faster,' she said.

I got up to thirty miles an hour and said, 'I'll tell you what. I bet we see an old bloke in a cardigan walking a dog. I'll bet your first year's family allowance.' She didn't reply; she knew I was rambling.

It's been a theory of mine for years, that: The Old Bloke With The Cardigan and Dog Theory. It started when I was a sixth-former and I used to go to the Corner Pin on a Friday Night and get legless on two and a half pints of Barnsley Bitter. Me and my mates would stagger home after midnight and no matter what the weather was we always saw a wizened old bloke in a cardigan walking a dog. We'd have competitions: who'd be the first one to spot him? Would he be walking towards Barnsley up Kendray Hill or away from Barnsley towards Stairfoot? What colour would his cardigan be? Would it be buttoned? If so, how many buttons? And, the clincher: would he speak and if he spoke, what would he say? We had a points system: if he said 'Evening' or 'Goodnight', we got five points. If he was aggressive and said something like 'Get on ooam before I crack yer' or 'You college lads shouldn't be drinking mucky beer', we got ten points, but the crowning glory, if Barnsley FC had been playing that night, was if he said the immortal phrase 'How's Barnsley Gone On?' Thirty points. Magic!

We drove up the road, past the garden centre, through Ardsley and towards Barnsley. We still hadn't seen him and, funnily enough, I was really wanting to see him. While I was at college I'd worked the old man and the dog into a kind of folk-myth: he protected Barnsley, I'd say to open-gobbed lasses from the Home Counties; he's like the lamplighter, I'd say, the night watchman, the guardian angel of a dirty northern town. Then I'd turn slightly away and vomit spectacularly onto a pile of books that always contained *The Catcher in the Rye* and *The Great Gatsby*. The girls from the Home Counties would leave the room and I'd be alone with an engineer from Stockport called Miles. The rich are different from us.

We drove into the hospital grounds. I was going to park in the car park but Lindsay told me you were allowed to drive up to the door. At the door we were put in a lift, whisked to a ward, details were taken, efficient nurses bustled about, and I felt out of it. I'd got a joke ready. If they said, 'Do you want to be there at the birth?' I was going to say, 'Well, I was there at the conception so I may as well go for the double!' but nobody asked me.

A little nurse who looked like Roy Barraclough took Lindsay off to a room. 'I'd like to be there,' I said, quietly; 'We'll call you when we're ready, Mr Matthewman,' said Roy. I walked over to the window: Barnsley was laid out, orange and black under the stars. I tried to recognise individual streets and imagined blokes with dogs and cardigans on each one. I became suddenly, unaccountably, worried. My mate Trev at school, he's got three, and he told me I'd suffer from The Sudden Worry. 'Just before it's born, Richard, you'll be sure that it'll come out with three heads and more legs than a hockey team but you'll convince yourself that you'll still love it.' I hadn't believed it before, but now I could feel it creeping over me.

After a while a nurse came and said, 'You can go and see your wife now, Mr er . . . Matthewman.' She led me into a little room; Lindsay was dressed in a sort of smock, sitting on the bed. There was a portable telly in one corner and a couple of paperback books on a shelf.

'They say it'll be a while yet; it could be the morning before anything happens,' she said.

I wandered over to the telly and switched it on. Son of Godzilla. A dinosaur was just hatching out of an egg. Scientists watched, their lips mouthing furious Japanese, but sounding American; the dinosaur wobbled out of the bits of eggshell and stood unsteadily. I turned it off. The Sudden Worry returned. When ours was born it would look like a triceratops.

The room, like all hospital rooms, was red hot. It reminded me of afternoons in my grandad's greenhouse, listening to his chest rattling like waves over shingle. I was sweating. In the rush to get dressed I'd just pulled a sweater on with nothing underneath, so I couldn't even take it off. I said to Lindsay, 'Are you OK if I just pop outside for a minute, get some fresh air?' She just waved me away, being there at the birth was for my benefit, not hers. I noticed a door marked 'Waiting Room', and pushed it open slowly. It was pitch dark. I felt along the wall for the light switch and turned it on. There was a mass cry of 'GEEOR!' and I came face to face with half a dozen Barnsley dads-to-be who had been trying to sleep on the chairs, the tables, and in one case, the floor. They all sat, stunned in the harsh light, trying to rub their faces off the front of their heads. One man, although he was fully dressed, was casting about for his clothes and mumbling, 'Ah didn't think ah were on days this week. Ah didn't think I were on days.' A big man with an NCB jacket on said, 'What is it then doctor? A lad or a lass. If it's a lad she'll kill me. She reckons Friday nights makes lads.'

I went out. Not everybody wanted to be present at the birth. I needed to get out. I forgot about the toilet and went down in the lift and walked out into the freezing air. The sweat dried on my brow and I began to shiver. I was nervous. More than that, I was terrified. My old life was going to end, here, tonight, December 9th 1981, and a new life was going to begin with responsibilities and nappies and sleepless nights and a baby that looked like a triceratops. I had to be calm, had to be strong, for Lindsay's sake.

Then I identified the source of my worry, admitted it, faced up to it: I hadn't seen the bloke with the cardigan and the dog. Daft as it seemed, I needed to see him, needed something to link the old life to the new life in the freezing December air.

I walked through the car park to the hospital entrance. I looked up and down the road, quickly. Nobody. A black taxi zoomed past with an old lady sitting in the back clutching a handbag. Overhead, an aeroplane rumbled through the clear sky, its lights flashing. I needed to go back to Lindsay, but I needed to see the bloke with the dog. It was like when I was little and I had to do things in a certain order on Saturday Night: first, have my bath and hair wash, then sit downstairs on the settee with my jamas and dressing gown on watching Richard Basehart in *Voyage to the Bottom of the Sea*, eating a bag of plain crisps and keeping as many of them in my mouth as I could before I swallowed any.

Suddenly, just as I was about to give up and go back into the steaming hospital, I saw him; the man with the dog and the cardigan. I couldn't believe it. I walked down the road towards him, just to make sure he was real, and his little Jack Russell barked at me. He looked at me like I was mad, or drunk, or both. 'Evening,' he said. And I recognised him! It was Flour-on-Hands! He used to work at the tennis-ball factory and he used to delight in telling us students about all the times during the day he and his wife made love. 'I once came up behind her while she were baking scones,' he said, 'and we did it there and then over the sink, and she still had flour on her hands!' We christened him Flour-on-Hands after that, although we never called him that to his face, and seeing him now, this night of all nights, linked all my past and my future together in a way I couldn't fathom.

'Flour-on-Hands!' I said. I couldn't remember his real name.

'What the hell are you on about?' he said. The Jack Russell was growling now.

'Richard Matthewman, tennis-ball factory, 1975,' I said. 'My wife's having a baby in there...' and as I pointed to the hospital lit up like a great ocean liner, I realised that that's where I should be, with my future, not my past, and I ran across the car park like my shoes were on fire.

They were just taking Lindsay into the delivery suite when I dashed out of the lift. 'Where've you been?' she shouted. 'It's OK, I've seen the man with the cardigan and the dog,' I said, but I knew she wasn't listening and I followed her into the room where new life began.

Just Like Ours Except for the Ducks

The man paid for the taxi in bags of ten pence coins. Ten quid in bags of ten pence coins and the driver never blinked. The man lugged his bag into the travel centre and bought a single to Cleethorpes. 'Eight quid,' said the ticket man. The ticket man needed a shave. The man took out his bags of ten pences.

On the platform the man stood in front of a chocolate machine and spoke to it in a loud voice. He said Give me your bastard chocolate. Nothing happened. He patted the ticket in his pocket. Then he patted it again. Then he slapped his pocket, then he thumped it hard. The ticket was still there.

On the train, the man seemed to relax. He looked out at the flat fields in the wasteland near Thorne. He tried to think.

Cleethorpes would be wonderful. The family would meet him. The two girls, pretty as pictures in their blue dresses. The little boy, he's a little rogue, walking now, straining against his reins. Shouting Daddy, maybe. Maybe all of them shouting Daddy and dancing a bastard jig. Maybe.

And the wife. The lovely wife, standing open armed. Smiling the kind of smile you dream about.

They would walk through Cleethorpes along the front and the children would say Daddy Daddy can we have this and can we have that and it would be as though the words were coming out of their mouths in little balloons like the balloons you see in comics. The words would hang in the air for him to hear and there would be no need to look at the words and make them out slowly and painfully. That would be lovely. And yes they could have that and yes they could have this. And out would come the bags of ten pences and there would be laughing and shouting and the little lad straining at his reins and the wife smiling her big smile and saying He's my man. Me and him, we're like this.

The train rolled into Scunthorpe and the man smiled. He knew one or two jokes about Scunthorpe. Really funny ones. Bastard killers. He'd tell them to the children, as they walked round Cleethorpes. The sun has got his bastard hat on. And they'd all laugh till they cried and the wife would smile her big smile and the sun would shine and make them sweat.

Outside Barnetby the train stopped. It sat there, humming.
The passengers stared out at clumps of trees and at a distant
farmhouse. The sun beat down and people used newspapers and
books to fan themselves. The driver climbed out of the train and
stood talking into a telephone by the line. The man looked out of the
window. This is not good is it? he said. This is not bastard good at
all. The woman opposite looked at her copy of the *People's Friend*.
Lends your paper, the man said. Lends it. The woman hurriedly
gave him the paper. He looked at it and gave it her back. I've read
that one, he said. It's next week's. Then he laughed.

He got up and walked down the train with his bag full of the
bags of ten pences. The train was almost empty. It sat there in the
heat. This is not good, he said. Then the train set off, and continued
by the squares of yellow rape.

After they had walked along the front they would go to the
caravan. The kiddies would be tired but happy. They would clutch
in their hot hands the things he had bought them from his bags of
ten pences. From his bags of ten pences and I bet the odd Irish one
and it doesn't matter when the sun shines out of a bastard clear blue
sky. The kids would fall asleep and their little eyes would shut and
they would look so peaceful. And the wife would smile her big smile
and they would go in the end bedroom and the walls would bastard
drip.

After that there would be the rest of their lives, like a tree. Like
the tree he used to see, changing with the seasons, growing bigger
and bigger, blocking out more light. More and more light. Some
great jokes about Scunthorpe.

That had been the first of the ten pences. He had broken into
the bag, broken into it to ring the house. And nobody in. So he had
rung his mother, and she had told him about Cleethorpes and the
van. And the children. And wouldn't it be better if. And he had said
Just you tell them to meet me and he had slammed the phone down
and the sow never knew bastard nothing anyway. Never made no
bastard sense at all.

Not far now. Big chemical works at Immingham pumping out
shit. None of your bastard shit must fall on the heads of my kiddies.

They would stand there, waving. All three kiddies and the little one straining at his reins. And the bags full of the ten pences in all the slots and the lights flashing and their little fists full of bastard belm.

The train rattled into Grimsby. Not far now, you ugly fat bastard, he said to a man walking past the train. Not far now.

He remembered what his mate had said. The mate who had been so close. The mate who read science fiction all the time until the lads said he was on bastard Mars all the time and the mate said No I'm not on Mars because there's no atmosphere there not like in this shitty hole.

Anyway the mate had said that he'd read a story about a bloke who said that there was a parallel world to this one and in this world everything was the same except that people walked about with ducks on their heads.

And the man had said Bastard ducks what are you about bastard ducks. And the mate, who was a bloody clever bloke, had said There is, according to this story, a parallel world where people walk about with ducks on their heads and it might be true it might not be bastard science fiction.

And the man had said That's rubbish that is pal, but secretly he took notice because the bloke was a clever bloke. Mind you he couldn't have been that clever or they wouldn't have caught him.

The train rolled into Cleethorpes station, and they would be there to meet him and the little one would strain at his reins and the girls in their dresses pretty as pictures and the wife smiling her big smile. He knew some really great jokes about Scunthorpe to make them smile and they would be waiting for him on the station.

The man got off the train and looked down the platform. There is this parallel world where the people are just like us except that they walk about with ducks on their heads. Some really great jokes about Scunthorpe.

On the Closure of Cadeby Colliery

'At first I heard a kind
of scrambling noise

then I heard a fluttering
and there was a bird

squeeze through, somehow,
the gas fire, the actual

gas fire, flapping about
behind the fireguard.

Your dad
was in the kitchen and...'

      I thought of how
      when the train stopped at Conisbrough Station
      you looked right and saw
      two lots of winding gear,
      how you looked left and saw
      two men demolishing Conisbrough Station.

      Oh and then I thought of how
      my dad worked on a farm in Lanarkshire
      and it was the 1930's and he joined
      the navy, and he saw flying fish
      'looking like bird and fish joined'
      and he'd seen nothing like it in Lanarkshire.

'...I ran in there with the kids and
anyway, he went home and

brought his landing net,
caught it, let it

go in the garden.
A bird in a landing net!'

Title (Northumberland June 11th/12th 1987)

Just notes really.
Nothing like real writing.

Profit is unpaid wages
The boys ran into the trees.

The girls cried.
Redraft the sand.
What is dad doing with

his shadow on the sand?
There is a new sign,
a footpath sign.
frightened, bud.
Redraft me, I am

Elizabeth holds up a cassette, spools
it out. 'I'm bandaging
the moon.'

Polling station.
Crowds of old people.
Lesbury village.

A Conservative landrover
with a flag flying
roaring through the streets
of Alnwick.
you are weeping Robin Day
weeping Peter Snow
And yes you are

Three A.M. The foghorn.
The day, redrafting itself.

The Flag

How do you paint te
rror?

Slow Thaw

My daughter tells me
of a dream she had.
'You were standing there'

What was I saying?
'Nothing.' What was I doing?
'Nothing.' Where was I?

'I had a dream.'
She stands at the window
looking out at the white

garden, at the footprints
that begin at the hedge
and go nowhere.

After a week of grey
the sky stretches blue
to breaking point.

She has forgotten the dream.
She shows me a painting
of someone in black.

And who is this? I ask,
pointing to a blue lump,
several red lines

in a corner. 'That's scribble'
she says, 'just scribble'
looking at me

as if I should know.

In Fear of Abstraction

The guard is small,
smaller than me.
'There's a failure
in front of us.
We don't know
when they'll move him'

he says. I stare
into the night,
into the night.
When I was small
I used to go into
the garden, saying

'I'm going to think'
and I used to walk
around the garden
in circles. Look:
an aeroplane,
low over Stockport,

small in the dark.
I've got a photo at home
of me when I was small,
laughing my bloody head off.
It's dark outside.
Down the train

the guard picks up
a small green shoe.
Look at the sky:
the aeroplane circling
around the dark,
into the dark.

Brief Encounter

He stood on the platform, and waved
at the disappearing words. I mean

he waved at the disappearing train.
A hand waved back from the words,

from the train I mean. He walked
into the cafe, into the room

where they had shared so much:
words (should I say, coffee) and words

(I mean food). His train waited on
the words or should I say his train

waited on the rails. He lingered
over his words, and a waiter

hovered, expecting payment, because
nobody had told him that words were free
or that they should be.

The Day after Armistice Day

Two men are jogging
in early morning light
by a canal.

I imagine
they are both
called Doreen,

which may seem
irrelevant,
but my memory

is locking
(with a click
audible

to the other passengers
on this crowded train)
into Doreen Parry

who keeps a shop
in Darfield
where I once bought a toy shotgun

for 8/11d.
So this is a poem
about disarmament,

not about jogging men
called Doreen.
Fooled you.

The Mirror in the Toilet

Some pieces are sharp
and some pieces
are very sharp. I've got
my hand in the toilet
and the water is freezing,
nearly frozen, and

there are bits of white
Andrex, little rolled bits,
among the sharp bits,
piling them on the frame

of the mirror. I just
walked out of the bathroom,
shut the door,
and the mirror fell off,
smashed in the toilet.
The water is so cold

that I have to stop and dry
my hands on an old
blue towel. I check my hands
for blood or splinters.
I hold them up to the light
and look at them, closely.

Essential Engineering Works

The train stops somewhere in the lit
midlands, sun reflecting . . . you know
the kind of thing I mean. The lit

midlands. Let me tell you some things
about this poem. This poem happens
on a train stopped in the midlands,

and this poem also happens, if a poem
can happen, in a gallery in Wales,
where a man is looking at photographs.

The two parts of this poem happen at once,
quickly, like the snap of a successful
christmas cracker. I am sorry; this poem

was meant to move more quickly to the
gallery in Wales from the lit midlands.
It is stuck on the line

somewhere between the midlands and Wales.
Listen, you can hear the poem's engine
running. It will start soon, it will

lurch into life. Essential engineering works
are holding the poem still; a man
is standing before a photograph, and he

is seeing only himself in the glass.
Listen, hear the poem's engine running.
Gaze at the photograph and wait, wait.

The er Barnsley Seascapes

1   Goldthorpe er Seascape

Park the car. Wind
the window down. Listen.
Shanties echoing
up the tight street

as the pitmen sing
their way from work.
The YTS lamplighter
stands, and his matches

cough out in
the well-trained wind.
He was not a clever
boy at school

so all he can say is
shit, not like us
clever people, who wind
the window down to catch

the dying tradition
on our Japanese tape recorders.
Shanties, clinking like
cardboard money,

the cardboard money
they have round here.
Burns easier.
Cheaper than coal.

2   M1 Seascape near Hoyland:
er it's a rough day

They huddle in their coats
and the gaffer holds his gun
but only for effect. For this
photograph I am taking, I suppose.

For the interview, the gaffer
is proud: 'We have only six more
miles of motorway to roll up
and dump in the sea' he quips.

3 · er Darfield Seascape

And the waves pound
against Clifton's shop
and Clifton's shop never closes.
On Christmas Day someone rushes in
for a pair of tights. She has
a bulging purse from Habitat
in the shape of a bath
filled with coal. Habitat coal,
silly bastard. Put it this way:
Darfield was mentioned in the Domesday Book.
Put it like this: a passing mention,
more of a mutter.

4   Little Houghton seascape er like

British Coal
sold the houses

made us live
in heads.

Great big
severed heads.

Rows of heads
overlooking the sea.

Sometimes I stand
in the eyes

and I cry.
Then I burn

the tears.
Cheaper than coal.

5   An old seadog er speaks

First it was called NCB, you'd see it
on the boats, then British Coal, on
the wharves, then they changed the name
to British A Vase of Flowers, changed all
the boats, all the wharves, all the
signs outside the pits, then they
changed it to British Very Nice
and a month later to British Smile
and they kept repainting the boats
the wharves the fish the seaweed the

6 er from a Learned Paper about the Seascapes

Very few of er the South Yorkshire
Coastal Mining Settlements survive
in anything like their original

er state. Some have become islands,
some have sunk into the sea, some
have worked loose from the earth

and slither around the countryside
scaring er owls and other woodland
creatures. One was found in Harrogate,

a town in North Yorkshire next to
the sea. 'It had er wings' said a local,
'and was tired from much hard flying'

7 Seaview Video, Barnsley: Er latest offers

Barnsley is Basingstoke!	£1.00 a night
Barnsley is Basingstoke 2!	£1.00 a night
The Cruel Sea (Remake)	£1.00 a night
Lost Horizon (Remake)	£1.00 a night
Barnsley is Japan!	£1.00 a night
Barnsley is Japan 2!	£1.00 a night

8 Seascape could er be anywhere around here

Only the water, solid
and glinting. Only
the noise of the water,

and the noise of the moon
slowly deflating, and
only the noise of the stars

being sold, clinking,
keeps me awake
all day.

The Christmas Tree's
Press Conference

No. I can't
reveal too much.

All storms are terrible.
This one, I agree,
was more terrible than most.

Yes, the baubles
suffered damage.

Yes, the angel
was lost.

No.

Gentleman at the back?

No. No, the tinsel
has always been this colour.

Don't

you like this colour?
Don't you like this colour?

Bastard? Shall I come over there
and kick shit out of you?

Bastard.

Sorry. I'm sorry.
It takes...a lot
out of one.

'The movement of the sea,
The deep, the deep,
    Holding you and me,
The deep'

as Belloc wrote.

The Grimness:
BBC Radio 4, Tuesday, 8.30 p.m.

We don't talk much
but when we talk
we talk about the Grimness.

Almost a cliché
in this muck.
Ah, The Grimness.
I remember it well.

And now on Radio 4
the poet Ian McMillan
presents a feature
on the Grimness of 1993
and what it did.

He talks to a number of people
who survived it
and some who
didn't.

Such a big microphone.

It just sort of sat there
on the settee.
Occasionally it looked at
the coffee table.
Sometimes it glanced
at a wedding photo.
Not its own.
Any wedding photo.
It
had
sacks
full.

Can you tell me something
anything about the Grimness.

Look at the view, kid.
Grimethorpe. The band
playing their lips out
but you can't hear them
because the window's shut.
It's smashed but at least it's
shut.

Grimethorpe. Is that mike on?
Is that thing turning?
You can't shift for Channel 4
film crews round here. Big fat bastards
with the arse crack showing, lugging
cameras. Thin kids with boom mikes.

You pick up the lingo.

Little lasses with clipboards.
The colliery band rushing
from shoot to shoot.

But the Grimness.
Can we talk about the Grimness?

In the sky, look. That constellation
there.
Round here we call it Wrecked Oil
Tanker,
that constellation, because there's no
shape
to it and it's black all around it.

Is that thing turning?
That's a joke.

O pinpoint the Grimness for me madam.
Pointpin it. Speak into this thing.
This, call it what you like, pimple.
Speak faster than you normally would
to compensate for my dying battery.
And in a higher register than you
would normally employ. Pin pin
the Grim? Point it?

The Grimness? Not a bad pub.
Dead tap room. Old caps with blokes under.
Knock of a domino echoing back from the '26 strike.
Scab's knock, you see. We pretended we didn't hear it.
It flies round the tap room like a bat. Nice lounge,
young people get in it. Just the one hairstyle
between them. They pass it round like drugs.
Big stuffed fish on the wall. Most pubs have a
big stuffed fish on the wall. Look at that one.
Look closely. Not a fish at all. Look.
A bird

in the shape of a fish. We're not daft.

There we have it. The Grimness. Grimethorpe 1993.
Defined. A miasma. The sticky bit of an envelope.
A burst h.w. bottle. Nelson: kiss me, Grimey.
Distant piccolo music. An ant's first breath.
Hooks in a butcher's trousers. I have polished my shoes.
Al Pacino in Carry On Grimethorpe. Valves. Sellotape.
Jiffy bag with a broken hen in it. Ten to four in the morning.

The Miner's Breakfast:

A bowl of Grimethorpe flakes. Look: a free model of Thunderbird
8, the forgotten one, like Ghandi, the tenth Marx Brother.

That's a short shopping list mister!
It's okay!
No shops!

Ian McMillan. BBC Radio 4. Grimethorpe.

Was that okay? Was my voice concerned enough? Enough about the Grimness? To be honest I wanted to laugh most of the time. It's funny. Do you think I should do that bit at the end again? Let's listen back. A man was trying to breathe in a house two miles away. Bloody deafened me pal.

Modernism: The Umbrella Girl
Forgets What She is Talking About

'The manufacture of Umbrella Frames and Tubes at Stocksbridge occupies...
300 workers, a majority of whom are girls...the finishing department is quite
a speciality of the gentler sex.' (C.H. Bird-David, 1910)

I'm talking about umbrellas.

I gitted, mainly. Summer afternoons I gitted,
until they put me on the ferrules
or the pinning in. Ivy gitted too,
and Florence, and Olive, and Nellie.

Hannah was on the japanning. The lacquer
stained her hands terrible. A man with
a dirty face is talking to a man
with a clean face. The taxi firm

is two doors away. I envy your fluidity.
The bodging was the worst. You had to
knock the lacquer out of the holes
in the ribs. They give you offals,

little leather caps to put on your
finger and thumb to save them
while you pressed the ribs
to test for strength. I think

I'd rather have a lion tear me to death
than a snake. I made a snake out of
plasticene. It crawled up my arm. Like eels.
When he brought eels I always said

Take them eels to Jimmy Hancock.

We are talking about eels.

Burst Pipe with 'A Level' Notes

Here I am, carrying	Narrator?
this empty kettle through a clear	Persona?
December night,	Winter of the Soul?
My Dad a few yards behind,	God/Christ?
my wife at home, mopping,	Madonna?
looking at the water	Sense of making whole?
coming through the ceiling.	Virgin birth?
That blinking red eye	Drink?
of the aeroplane	Idea of Heaven?
We see every night at this time	Eternity?
and that girl	Made-up?
with the made-up face	Pun on Fiction?
collecting the Avon	Scavenger?
catalogues. Ding Dong.	Doorbell?
Face framed in the door.	Like a portrait?
Every time I ring	Prayer?
the plumber's mobile phone	Plumber = God?
he doesn't answer it.	Church and state?
When he left our house	Desertion by God?
he said he was going	Looking into darkness?
to look into a loft.	Severed head?
I fill the kettle	Family life?
at my mother's. She gives	Bacon?
me some bacon.	Is God dead?

Halifax!

History nags like a mouth
ulcer, and you can't tell
where one year starts
and the other one ends

except the slang gets
further away from words
you understand. Hunk,
dish, pillock you grew

up with, streets of them.
Now bevs pull bleeds
and you shout Halifax!
I made that last one up.

History nags like a mouth
bleeding, a dream
you can't remember
and therefore never had,

a film you never saw
but read the reviews of
and they were all bad,
they were all bad.

Halifax! History nags
like a mouth, History smells
like a DSS-approved hotel,
a waiter with a tie on elastic,

a receptionist drinking
lager through a straw
who tells you No Messages
Halifax! I'm on this late

night bus, alone except for
a hunk, a dish and a pillock
with a mouth ulcer, throbbing
like history with batteries.

It's my stop. I'll get off.
Invent some new slang. Halifax!
Canvey! Oban! Barnsley!
Dursley! Chester le Street!

Rotherham

Rotherham's always been an exotic place to me. I live near Barnsley, about six miles from here, and before the invention of the M1 we used to drive through Rotherham on empty Sunday afternoons to visit my Auntie Mabel on the outskirts of Clowne. We'd drive through impossibly unworldly places like Greasbrough, Halfway and Swallownest. There's a street in Greasbrough called Harold Croft and I knew a man in Barnsley called Harold Croft. Impossible, unworldly. It's a little terrace just down the hill from the taxidermist. My dad would sing 'Roll Along Covered Wagon Roll Along', my brother would be asleep with his head lolling, and my mother would be checking her face in the vanity mirror. That was then, this is now. I'm in Rotherham trying to forget my cosy 1960s pictures of the place, and trying to find some 90s images. Here's one: the discarded rubber band on the floor. They're everywhere, not just in Rotherham. Britain is covered in rubber bands. We know they're really dropped by postmen, but they're sinister. They're rubber bands from the sky, bendy shapes from hell, people turned into rubber bands when we're not looking. Harold Croft: street in Greasbrough, man in Barnsley, rubber band near Rotherham Library. Here's another image, wrapped round this fence near Rotherham central station: the wrecked cassette, the tape flapping in the wind. You see them everywhere: hanging from trees, waving from barbed wire fences, coiling along the floor beside a couple of rubber bands. Is this it, then for Rotherham? For the North? From travel through uncharted parts called Halfway to a bit of rubbish on a mucky floor? By Rotherham Central Station I sat down and wept? We once came on a school trip to Rotherham when I was an infant. Sixty of us on one Burrows Bus, still dusty from taking the early shift to Darfield Main. All the way, people kept saying, 'Watch out for that Lion, he'll have thi.' I had lettuce sandwiches with salad cream and I was worried because Peter Wake had said, 'Lions Like Lettuce'; I knew really that there weren't any Lions in Rotherham because I'd looked for them on my way back from Auntie Mabel's the week before and not seen any. We walked into Clifton Park museum and there, in the entrance, was the biggest lion I'd ever seen. Stuffed, one paw aloft. I wept, and held Mrs Hinchcliffe's hand tight. The bus driver, Biv Burrows, walked up to the glass and tapped it boldly. 'It's okay, kid,' he said, 'I think it's dead.' The lion's still there. Go and see it next time you're in Rotherham. And Peter Wake was wrong: it doesn't like lettuce, it likes rubber bands and cassette tape. Don't be frightened. I think it's dead.

Snails on the West Shore, August 1991

It had been raining, and my son
wanted to see the snails. We ran
out of the guesthouse, long before breakfast,

our feet brushing the owner's *Telegraph*
in the hall where the paperboy had left it,
almost stepped on the face of John McCarthy,

blinking in the light of the world's flash,
and we ran towards the Gogarth Abbey Hotel
where Alice Liddell stayed as a little girl,

Alice in Wonderland waiting inside her
like the idea of a butterfly waits inside
a picture of a caterpillar. My son

did his usual trick, running like mad
at a gang of gulls, laughing as they
climbed the sky, landed on the roof

of the Gogarth Abbey Hotel. Then we began
to see the snails, far more than yesterday,
dozens of them, punctuating the damp path

like they owned it, slowly, so slowly,
from the wall to the road. My son
stopped, his three-year-old head

focusing down to the snails moving slow
as the low clouds that hung over the Orme.
He stared at the snails, the slow old man

inside him waiting like the idea of a bird
waits inside the picture of an egg. Down past
the Gogarth Abbey Hotel a gull swooped down

on a snail, bashed it on the floor, rose
towards the Orme's clouds and the grey sky.
My son was frightened, looked down

at the snails crossing the path, looked up
at the gulls slicing the sky's silence, looked
at me, saw the boy I once was, the slow

old man I would become, crossing paths
in a grey winter. Later, in the residents'
lounge, he laid his cars out in a long line;

'Is it a traffic jam?' I asked. 'It's snails
crossing the path,' he said. I bent down
to pick one of the cars up. 'Leave it,'

he said, 'It's a snail crossing the path.'
I looked up, saw John McCarthy on the tv,
blinking in the light of the world's flash,

thought of how we must learn to live together;
snails, young boys, fathers, and the slow
old men they must become, under the Great Orme

and the clouds dark as a cell door.

Three Boring Miles on the Exercise Bike

Three boring miles. The television flickering
in the corner of my eye. A man talking.

The view doesn't alter, of course. The rain
coming down steadily, Joe's grandma

taking him down to school, coming back again.
Mile one. The speedometer hovering

around twelve. So in an hour I could be
almost in Sheffield, halfway to Leeds,

my legs going slowly, slowly, going nowhere,
my wife lifting the same cup of coffee

to her lips for mile after mile, the steam
pulling away from the cup like smoke,

a man talking. It's me, saying the same things
over and over again. Mile two. The phone rings,

I pedal, my wife answers it again and again.
It's the same bad news, pulling away like smoke,

Joe's grandma taking him to school.
She waves this time. She waved last time.

Her glasses are the same as they have been for years.
My view doesn't change. A window of trees,

rain, Joe's grandma, my wife, the cup of coffee,
the telephone, the bad news, my legs going slowly,

slowly, in an hour I could be halfway to here,
almost into this room, the room pulling away

like smoke from a dying fire. Mile three.
The view doesn't alter. A man talking. It's me.

Smoke

It started with a dream:
she wore smoke, she wore a wide skirt,
she was a slow dancer, lived in the North
she

and it continued with a walk,
early Sunday morning, to get out
of the house that pressed
like a flannel. Like a flannel
on a mask.

Smoke. Grey smoke from
a burning chimney
in a smokeless pit village.

The dream:
I look good in blue, like the sea.
I look good in black, like the night.

I dream poems. When I try
to write them they are just

smoke. Time cracked. March
in Summer, Christmas a long
cool drink with a slice of lemon.

I think that's what the dream said.
I scribbled it down in the dark.

Anyway, how does the blind man know
when his paper is dirty?

If you see what I mean.

Bosnia Festival:
Your Full Guide by our Arts Reporter

At 10.00 a.m. mime show
by The Shuffling Headscarves.
Nothing much happens;
some shuffling, weeping.
Mimed weeping, that is.

At Midday, cabaret
in The Bread Queue
by The Arguing Headscarves.
Nothing much happens;
a feeble argument. Behind them
The Ducking Headscarves
are ducking the snipers.
The Shuffling Headscarves
mime weeping.

At three p.m. a one man show
by a man in a white suit
talking into a camera.
Nothing much happens.
The Shuffling Headscarves, The
Arguing Headscarves and the Ducking
Headscarves continue their act

which one critic described
as a lot of shuffling, arguing
and ducking.

There's so much happening.
There's almost too much to take in.
A kind of festival fatigue
comes over you: all these headscarves,
all that weeping, all those gestures.

Godot turned up last night, by the way,
in a headscarf, weeping.

The actors stood with their mouths open
like fish. Fish on a bloody slab.

The 70. What a wonderful bus that was; Sheffield to Upton. I never went as far as Upton (did anybody?) but I often went from Darfield to Sheffield and back, to Pink Floyd concerts at the City Hall, to the Cineplex to see *The Life and Times of Judge Roy Bean*, to the bookshops on Chapel Walk. A whole cultural education defined from the top deck of a bus that seemed to turn every corner, go down every side street, and wait unaccountably at Wombwell Baths for ages.

The route: I'd get on at Darfield Ring. It would be the early 70s, say 1972. The Darfield Urban District Council men would be putting plants in the middle of the roundabout. One of them would be sucking a tomato. He always sucked a tomato. Up Nanny Marr Road, down Snape Hill Road, past Low Valley Juniors, my old school, past Darfield Main and into Wombwell. A lot got off in Wombwell, especially if it was Market Day. I wished that I could get off and run to Grace's van for an ice-cream, but there was never time. Then up to Wombwell Baths where my dad would take me on a Saturday morning to teach me to swim. He didn't succeed. The long wait. Sometimes the driver switched the engine off. Kids with towels and wet hair would get on and sit there shivering. Then up Hough Lane and instead of going up Wood Walk we'd turn left; one hour we'd turn left and go to Hemingfield, other hours we'd turn left and go into Jump. ('Is this bus going to Jump? Well hold it down while I get on.') Then the indefinable lanes around Hoyland and Elsecar, chugging up and down hills past pubs, schools, shops, more pubs. Past the NCB Workshops at Elsecar. We didn't know that in twenty years the NCB Workshops at Elsecar were going to be the centre of Barnsley's burgeoning tourist industry. We weren't that clever. Down into Chapeltown. A lot on, a lot off. Another wait. Then up the hill towards Ecclesfield and the cruel trick that your brain always played was that you thought you were almost there; you'd left the Barnsley pits (Darfield Main, the recently closed Wombwell Main, Elsecar, Barrow, the one at Platts Common, Smithy Wood) behind and you were entering the Metropolis. You weren't. Through Ecclesfield. Past an opticians. Past a club called the Limes. To Lane Top. Down towards the Wicker. Almost there now. The windows would be steamed up and you'd be feeling a bit bilious. Then into Pond Street, and off to the City Hall, the Pictures, the Bookshops.

I still can't drive, and I sometimes catch the 70 into Wombwell from Darfield. Except it's not called the 70 anymore, it's the 271, and it's not a huge double decker, it's a little minibus called a Town Link. I don't think it's possible to get from Sheffield to Upton anymore by public transport without an overnight stay. Maybe I'll try it sometime.

Frog Dream

great moon, hopping
sky: pond
great moon
like the time before legs
great moon
rolling at memory's
pond edge
great moon, singing
croaking in the froglight
huge frog's head
hanging in the sky

Dear Mr McMillan

Dear Mr McMillan,
      My cousin tells me that you are the writer of a humorous column in the *Sheffield Telegraph*. I wonder if you would be interested in hearing about a funny thing that happened to me in June of 1963? I myself have not read your column but I used to enjoy Cassandra in the *Daily Mirror*.

Yours sincerely, Mr A B of Gleadless.

Dear Mr A B,
      Many thanks for your letter. Yes, I'd love to hear about the funny thing that happened to you in 1963. I'm always looking for material for my column. I'm too young to remember Cassandra myself!

All the best, Ian McMillan.

Dear Mr McMillan,
      As requested I am writing with details of the incident that happened to me in 1963, in the hope that it will be of interest and amusement to your readers. It took place on the evening of June 4, as my wife and I were enjoying a quiet evening at home. I was boiling the kettle for the Ovaltine when I heard my wife shout from the front room. I went into the front room and there to my surprise I was greeted by the very humorous sight of my wife sitting on the floor with a small to medium pile of soil on her head. What had happened was that my wife was standing on a stool (or a chair, I forgot which) to put a potted plant on a high shelf on our display unit and had slipped from the stool (or chair) thus bringing the plant pot onto her head. Well I can tell you we had a good laugh about it.

Yours sincerely, Mr A B of Gleadless.

Dear Mr A B,
      Many thanks for sending me the story of the plant pot falling on your wife's head. Although it made me smile a bit, I don't know if it would be funny enough for my readers who are used to a pretty

side-splitting standard! Perhaps you could tell me some more funny stories from your life?

All the best, Ian McMillan.

Dear Mr McMillan,

I was most disappointed to learn that you will not be able to use the funny story of the plant pot falling on my wife's head because it is not funny enough for your readers. I can assure you that my wife and I have laughed about it for many years now, on and off. Mind you, I did send it to Cassandra in 1966, and heard no more about it, despite SAE.

Perhaps your readers will be interested in a remarkable coincidence that happened to me in 1973?

Yours sincerely, Mr A B of Gleadless.

Dear Mr A B,
Yes, please do send me details of the remarkable coincidence.

All the best, Ian McMillan.

Dear Mr McMillan,

As requested I am sending you details of the remarkable coincidence that happened to me in 1973. Every year my wife and I have a week in Cleethorpes at the Sea View Guest House. You can imagine my surprise when in 1973 the couple at the next table, a haulage contractor and his wife, were called Mr and Mrs Gleadless! I trust that this amazing but true coincidence will amuse and interest your readers. If you don't want to use it, throw it away. I sent it to Cassandra in 1974 but he said that he lost it.

Yours sincerely, A B of Gleadless.

A Cliché Defines the Moment in a Poem about Language and Oppression

A blackened Yorkshire pit village
in the smoke
of a burning chimney, 1968;

Joan always burned her chimney
Sunday Mornings,
heating the oven for the Yorkshires.

'Yorkshire's finest Yorkshires!'
cried Joan, a pinny
on legs. Her husband George

smiled and smiled,
cracking his blue scars, and said
'You've hit the nail on the head!'

> Outside, tall Sarah
> and her husband Sam
> new from Ayrshire, and a
> pit shut as a cellar door,
> listening at the window,
> pulled to Yorkshire
> by the NCB's smiling promises
> and a film called *King Coal*.

Rows of houses like rows of boots.

> Sarah leaned towards
> the open window,
> caught the end of the phrase
> '...nail on the head!'

and smiled and smiled and said
'It's okay, Sam; they use clichés like we do'
and Sam leaned in the open window
like a sailor through a porthole and said
'You've hit the nail on the head!'

And they all smiled, like skulls smile.

Mining Town

As he goes to sleep
my son's face loses definition.
He becomes like the Man
in the Moon, or a child's
drawing of a face.

His eyes flicker. Outside, in
the light of a Summer evening
Mr Johnson bends down, picks leaves up,
only really he's looking for his wife
who died at the start of the year.

If I think hard I can recall her face just.
My daughters are talking about their visit
to the Yorkshire Mining Museum.
They went right to the face. It was
like a child's drawing
of a moonless night.

And that's it, really. This place
has gone down like a balloon,
one of those balloons that you find
behind the settee two weeks after Christmas.

Nothing more to say. I find it hard
to imagine my dad as a boxing champ;
he was, though, in the Navy, in the 1940s.
He's so gentle. I imagine him saying sorry
every time he punched somebody.

'I never went for the face'
he told me once.

A Discussion on Modern Poetry with Example: Postman Pat's Suicide Note

1   I like Blanka best, the way
he electrifies all the others.
Chun-Li is pretty good
and her Spinning Bird Kick

is astonishing, especially
in the six-button arcade version
like the one we played
on the Ferry. E. Honda

is good, too; we call him
Fat Eddie. He moves fairly
slowly, though, and his fat
never wobbles. Dhalsim's arms

and legs make me gasp, the way
they elongate. Ryu is deep.

2   Up and down the same hills
through the same weather
over and over, and that tune
only in my head
not in Ted Glen's.

All the birds are singing
and the day is just
the day.

Bar Wars

Pull up a comfortable chair, friend. Thrown another burn-effect log on the log-effect fire, and I'll tell you a story. A story of human endeavour and passion, of cunning and stealth. A story of signwriting. I call the story Bar Wars, and I'm hoping to sell it to a Hollywood producer for a 27-figure sum. I've changed all the names to protect the innocent.

It all started a few months ago on the busy main road near our house. The road is dead straight, they told us at school it was Roman, and there are two big lay-bys within a few hundred yards of each other at the same side of the road.

One day, a caravan appeared in one of the lay-bys. A small touring caravan behind a Volvo estate. On the caravan were the words SNACK BAR and TEAS. It said JANET'S on the front, and on the back, for some reason, it said HOT N COLD. For a couple of days nothing happened because they're mighty suspicious folk round these parts. Then I began to notice the occasional car parked up, the odd truck. Inside the cab of the truck I would see a huge man making short work of a bacon sandwich the size of Rutland. I peeped into the caravan a few days later as I passed the full lay-by. Janet herself presided over a table surrounded by truckers, reps, and mysterious chaps who might have been spies. Janet rang a noisy till and slept easily in her bed, her dreams full of gently sizzling sausages and vehicles slowing down and coming to a halt.

Christmas approached. A man needs a good breakfast inside him. Janet added the word BREAKFASTS to the side of the little caravan and men queued at the door, lorries hooted as they went by, and Janet's name was famous from Dover to Wick. Janet put a tiny Christmas tree in the window of the caravan and on Christmas Eve all the truckers and reps and mystery men got a free mince pie with their whopping breakfasts.

The year turned into a new decade and Janet's trade stayed steady. Then the unthinkable happened: a rival caravan parked in the next lay-by. A lugubrious bloke with a face like a comic's straight man stood on a set of rickety steps and wrote on the caravan in thick black felt tip: TURNER'S TEA BAR. It took him days.

Janet shrugged him off. Her lay-by stayed full. Turner sat in his caravan, looking like a bereaved basset hound, gazing at the cars and lorries and vans and trucks zooming by to Janet's home comforts. Then Turner hit on a new strategy: signs at the side of the road. I pictured him in my mind's clear eye sitting bolt upright in bed and shouting: 'SIGNS AT THE SIDE OF THE ROAD!' He put two up, one at either side of the road, quite near his lay-by. TURNER'S TEA BAR, they read, NEXT LAY-BY. And he began to get customers. The odd one or two, to start with. Then three, and four. Where before Janet had eight customers and Turner had none, it became Janet six, Turner two; then Janet four, Turner four, and once or twice four-all. So Janet fought back: fire with fire. Two signs, at the side of the road, just in front of Turner's: JANET'S BREAKFASTS. And two cunning signs a good half mile before the lay-bys: JANET'S BREAKFASTS.

Turner wasn't going to take this lying down. No siree. Two more signs, a mile away from the lay-bys: TURNER'S TEA BAR, ONE MILE.

That was last week. It's neck and neck, no quarter asked, none given. It's a fight to the death. The market will only stand so much; there are only so many breakfasts a man can eat.

And now the pub down the road is displaying a sign: BREAKFAST FROM 5AM. Watch out for a bleary-eyed spring on the old Roman road.

Sonny Boy Williamson is Trying to Cook a Rabbit in a Kettle

Ingredients:

1. Rabbit
2. Water

Method:
1. Attempt to get lid off kettle.
2. Attempt to get lid off kettle.
3. Attempt to put rabbit in kettle.
4. Use harmonica to squeeze rabbit in kettle.
5. Switch kettle on.
6. Settle down to watch *My Friend Flicka* on huge black and white 1960s hotel TV.
7. Inspect kettle. Trouser press switched on by mistake.
8. Take toast out of trouser press and eat it. Tastes of trousers.
9. Switch kettle on.
10. Settle down to watch *My Mother The Car* on huge black and white 1960s hotel TV.
11. Smell burning.
12. Hit top of TV with harmonica.
13. Smell burning.
14. Attempt to put burning kettle out with small plastic 1960s containers of hotel milk.
15. Run from the room shouting I TRIED TO COOK A RABBIT IN A KETTLE BUT THE KETTLE CAUGHT FIRE.
16. Realise that's a catchy tune.
17. Sing it: I TRIED TO COOK A RABBIT IN A KETTLE BUT THE KETTLE CAUGHT FIRE…

The Scream on Stockport Station

She is carrying the scream
through the darkness.

That head like a Mazda bulb
I'd know it anywhere.

She is carrying the scream
through the station.

That face like a turnip lamp from hell
I'd know it anywhere.

She is carrying the scream
past the buffet

That head like a dying balloon
I'd know it anywhere.

She's brought it home from Norway
to stockport

to a little house in stockport
where the person it's a portrait of

is screaming with happiness.

My Caravan's Got a Bontempi Organ in it

I drive my caravan slowly
up the A1.
I like to look at the view.

I drive my caravan very slowly
up the A1.
I like to compose songs about the view

because my caravan's got a bontempi organ in it.

I park my caravan carefully
in the field.
I like to be near the water.

I park my caravan very carefully
in the field
I like to be near the other caravanners

because my caravan's got a bontempi organ in it.

I play my bontempi organ at night
under the stars
and all the other caravanners sing along.

I play my bontempi organ all through the night
under the beautiful stars
and all the other caravanners
and sometimes, it seems,
the stars and the moon,
sing along:

O stars like fine pimples
on the sky's face
o moon like a turnip
a white one
let the sounds of my organ
drift into space
till the dawn
pulls skywards
the sun

because my caravan's got a bontempi organ in it.

The Ice House

Every Sunday afternoon we used to go on our Sunday afternoon run. There were two routes. Route one: from Darfield via Goldthorpe to Hickleton with its churchyard with the skulls in the gate, turn left at Hickleton crossroads for a Danny's ice cream, then past Bilham Sand quarry to Hooton Pagnell, described by Arthur Mee in his *Counties of England* as a Jewel in a sea of coal, then past the mysterious church in the middle of a field at Frickley and back home. Route two: through Darfield to Millhouses, turn left at Holly House, the old pit owner's house where the beekeeper lived, through Middlecliffe, once called Plevna, and Great Houghton, past Houghton Woods to a Danny's ice cream at Brierley Crossroads. A childhood of Sundays dominated by mysterious buildings and Danny's Ice Cream. And my dad would always say the same things as we drove along. Past a house at the edge of Great Houghton he'd point and say 'We now pass the famous house of Dick Turpin, famous for his horse Black Beauty. And now we approach the ducky pond, famous for the ducks.'

And for all those years of Sundays as we sat at Brierley Crossroads eating ice cream, I never knew this place was here: the ice house, deep in the woods that the man at Burntwood Hall created for his pleasure. A treasure under the ground, melting away.

Epic, I Mean an Epic Feel to it

What happened was that I was making the fire,
screwing up the paper, about to put the firelighters in

and one of the firelighters, a cheap firelighter,
crumbled over my trousers; soft, precise light dust

sprinkled on the black cords like stars in the night sky
over Wombwell during the dream I had on Sunday night, the one

where all the lights of Wombwell died in their sleep, except that
one. I tried to, but couldn't, force myself to sleep. Dawn

was in the dream, walking through Wombwell towards a fire
flickering just behind the Pico snack bar. I lit the fire,

brushed the firelighter from my trousers. The light.
I haven't told you which one didn't go. Which light.

It doesn't matter. I might have the same dream tonight,
the one where Wombwell is bathed in a version of night

that includes a couple of elements of day: sleeplessness,
and restlessness. Dawn suffers badly. From sleeplessness.

Grace

died, slumped
in her ice-cream van
on Wombwell market.

It's like New York City
some days at that crossroads.
I mean the traffic,

I mean the indifference.
Mr Spencer
at the Spencer Sewing Centre

hangs a tape measure
around his neck
wears it an inch longer each year

from the right
to the left. Time passes.
Like new York City,

I mean the high buildings,
I mean the indifference.
Grace knitted, slack times,

Decembers in her van.
I mean the cold,
I mean the indifference.

Mr Spencer, late December,
pulls an inch
moving closer to Grace.

Top Row/Low Row, Woolley Colliery Village

We used to say
Meet you at The Green Hut,

See you at the top
of Low Row, by the third

lamp post, him that works,
lightheaded. We used to say

I can't hear the motorway now,
you get used to her, I can't hear

the chips frying in The Green Hut
like I used to. Open every teatime.

We used to say Get off up to school,
never mind staring out of the window,

plenty of time for staring later.
We used to say

They need lights on that path,
We used to say I like the lights

on that path, we used to say
the lights on that path

are going to get broke.
Meet you at The Green Hut.

See you at the bottom
of Top Row. We used to skip

   Top Row, Low Row,
   Mucky washing on show.

Vests and white pants, flapping
in the wind from Russia, lightheaded.

George and Joe on a Bench:
Wind-Symmetry

George, from Windhill,
hair permanently shocked
into a bush. A real bush.

Joe, Low Row,
face folded over itself,
into a slice of bread. A real slice.

> On a dark night
> in his garden
> George could be a window.
> On a dark night
> in his house
> Joe could be a wall.

On this bench
they could be twins.
Twin candles, twin snowmen
melting into different shapes.

That kind of twin.
That k. of t.

Brisk Coffee

I got an early train from Sheffield to Leeds the other day, then I had to wait for a connection, so I found myself in the buffet at 7.30 a.m., clutching a steaming medium coffee and staring at my fellow passengers. It's not that I'm nosey: I'm a writer, and that's the kind of thing writers are supposed to do.

It was the usual buffet cross-section, I guess: men with birds tattooed on their muscular necks, couples gazing hungrily at each other, elderly ladies glancing incessantly from side to side, and a few impossibly glamorous young things who must have got up at about half past three to end up looking like that at 7.30 in Leeds.

Then a man walked in, or should I say then a man walked in *briskly*. He was a brisk businessman in a brisk suit with a brisk hairdo. He did everything briskly: he strode across to the table nearest the counter and put his top-opening briefcase down on it. He went to the counter and ordered a small coffee from the lad with lav brush hairstyle. The lad snapped a lid on the coffee and old Brisky shovelled up a few sachets of sugar. He went back to the table, prised the lid off the coffee and poured the contents of a couple of sachets of sugar into the brownish liquid. People looked at him curiously. He was more interesting to look at than the sandwiches. He stirred the coffee with a biro which he wiped briskly with a white hanky. He did not put the lid back on the coffee. He put the cup of coffee carefully into the top-opening briefcase. He snapped the briefcase shut. He strode away, swinging the briefcase jauntily.

The rest of us, the early morning buffet crowd, all stared after him then stared hard at the lid, motionless on the white formica table. He walked out of the station. He hailed a taxi by waving his briefcase in the air.

He's been haunting me ever since, that bloke. It was a momentary lapse of reason, I suppose. A little explosion in the head that makes you forget to do the things that you do so often they become instinctive, like zipping your fly up or opening the door before you walk through it. Every day he gets his coffee at 7.32. Every day he puts the lid on. But not that particular day. All week I've been speculating on why and what next?

Maybe he jumped from his taxi, sprinted into the boardroom. The boss looked up, stern as God over his half-moon glasses. 'Have you got those important documents, George?' the boss says in a voice like cracking ice. 'You mean the documents that must stay dry at all costs?' says George. 'Yes, I mean the documents that must on no account get wet,' creaks the boss. George reaches into his briefcase...

Or maybe he wasn't a businessman at all, but a spy. Maybe that quiet middle-aged woman flicking through the *People's Friend* over there by the door of the buffet was his contact. Maybe the sign to quit the safe house (you can tell I read a lot of spy novels) was the lidless coffee in the coffee-coloured briefcase. Come to think of it, she did leave soon after, leaving her *People's Friend* flapping on the table, open at a story called 'Love by the side of Loch Eck'.

Or maybe he wasn't a businessman or a spy. Maybe he was just eccentric. Maybe he'd had enough. Seize the day. No more boring old George, doing the same thing every day. The coffee in the briefcase was just the start of it. Later he'd dress up as Rasputin and startle the typing pool. Later still he'd sit in the canteen with a fake plastic hatchet in his head.

If you're reading this, George, can you let me know?

Sunset ovver Barnsley

Sithi, it were red
as red as that singlet
tha kept wearing last Summer,

as red as them tomatoes
thi fatha grew in his greenhouse
we had cartloads on em last Summer,

as red as thy face
when tha got mad wi him on't telly
tellin kids ow ter talk,
red as a rose in Summer,

gret fat fadin sunset
blood orange
ovver Barnsley
red as the way we speyk

The Next Poem I Write

The first verse: will have the woman in it, the woman standing in the school staffroom, as the school secretary tapes a science programme from the radio. Those schools radio presenters have a certain kind of voice. The woman will be showing the school secretary her personal alarm. It would make a noise if she was attacked. The woman says, 'When you've been brayed up by a bloke it toughens you up.' The school secretary says, 'I can eat what I like and I don't get fat.'

The second verse: will have that school party in it, rushing for their bus, rushing past me as I walked round Worsbrough Res. Those white haired twins, walking at the back of the group. Two boys, alike. White hair.

The third verse: will have the butcher in it that I saw running down the road. His apron was a striped red. It will also have a question in it: why do so many butchers shops have clocks in?

Postmodernist Summer Nights
in the Dearne Valley

Went to see a blues band
called the Pete Mitchell Smith
Blues Band at the Thurnscoe Hotel,
missed the last 212, walked home.

Contemplated school names
resonating like boat names
or the names of fishing flies:
Springwood, Upperwood, The Hill,

Low Valley, Sacred Heart, Lacewood.
I've got conjunctivitis. Entropy
and collapse by the Coronation Club,
turn on, attracting more, many more

than the Pete Mitchell Smith
Blues Band. Language falls in
on itself. A dead fish falling
in the bath. I know this valley

like the back of my hand. Look
at the back of my hand. It's
a mystery to me. A mystery.
Your dad's gone fishing.

On his own.

The Literary Life

This is what happened. All my family got this stomach bug, from the baby to the four-year-old to the six-year-old to the wife. Meanwhile, I'm in Frankfurt, representing British Poetry at a Festival of British Writing. I get home, home is the hero, bags of duty free gifts and little knick-knacks, and there's the family, laid out, being sick in waste-paper bins, weeping, shaking their little fists.

So all the duty frees go in a pile on the floor and I'm on mopping-up duty, jet-lagged, still quivering from that little pocket of turbulence we hit over the channel when my stomach turned upside down and it felt like my feet were coming through my eyes.

Gradually the family get better. The duty frees and the little knick-knacks get distributed and then of course the stomach bug flies around the room, hits a bit of turbulence over the microwave, and lands on me, home is the hero. The bug sits on my shoulder and says Right, I'll get you in a minute.

This is how it happened. They're all better, I'm feeling fine. I have to go to Wakefield to meet an Important Man in the Arts. We meet in a Pizza Hut, that's how important he is. As I walk in, the bug says (in a Vincent Price voice) Now is The Time, and slips inside my stomach. I hardly notice a thing. Except I start to sweat. And I start to yawn. My brow is like a watering can, my palms are leaking all over the menu. The Important Man in the Arts notices this. He says, 'Are you feeling okay?' and I say 'Is it warm in here or is it just me?' Then he says something very profound and important and I yawn a great big Jaw Cracker. I think maybe it's hunger pangs so I start to eat the pizza and the bug unpacks its suitcases and starts to hang its family portraits on my stomach wall.

I have a pudding. By this time my face is like Victoria Falls and I can hardly keep awake. Whatever the Important Man in the Arts says I just nod at. Very slowly. The bug plays football in my stomach, then it plays rugby, then lacrosse, then cricket then basketball. We leave the Pizza Hut. I'm staggering like a man who's had 15 pints. It's like turbulence: my feet feel like they're about to come through my eyes.

Somehow I get home. Home is the hero, looking like a man who's been swimming with his clothes on. During the meal my biro burst in my pocket, so I've got Dadaist patterns all over my shirt. I think that I can defeat the bug by sheer willpower. I loll in agony on the settee, summoning up willpower. The bug laughs its head off in my stomach.

Unpleasant things happen in the bathroom. I won't go into them. The sun glints on the sink, the childrens' toys have an innocent air, certain sounds can be heard. I summon up willpower, it doesn't work. I feel like a child of three.

I go to bed, can't be bothered to shut the curtains, can't be bothered to get undressed, leave me alone, ink from the burst biro all over my shirt, socks itching.

Suddenly it's the middle of the night. I'm hot. The bed appears to be full of rubble. The baby is in bed with us, snoring loudly. He sounds like a JCB. I toss and turn, turn and toss. Find that I feel slightly better if I lay on my back and lift up my left leg. It seems to help. The bug attacks me with a lump hammer. I get out of bed, sweating like a melting snowman. Downstairs its cool. Nice and cool. I sit on the settee, just for a minute. I'll be all right in a minute. Leave me alone. Print all over one side of my head. I fall asleep, have two dreams.

First dream: I'm at the side of the road. It's misty. A strange glass ambulance comes past. It's full of brides and grooms looking out, waxy. Second dream: I hail a taxi. It stops. I give the driver a teapot. 'Can you take this to my house?' I say.

I wake up. Where am I? On the settee. Rough cushion, my face all creased. Creased on one side, print on the other. My wife comes in. It's morning. 'You've got a column to write,' she says. This is what happened.

The Continuity Girl has Died

Came in through the door
in a red hat, came through
the door in a blue hat,
stick in the right hand,

the left hand, the one
with the ring, the one
without the ring, the sense
of loss obvious in the

breaking face, the smile
lighting the room, the tears
cascading like bath water,
the grin big banana under

the blue hat, black hat,
red hat, no hat, stick
in this hand or that hand,
the socks plain, patterned,

the chin bristling, the chin
smooth, shaved, unshaved,
gleaming under the blue hat,
red hat, stick, no stick,

tears, smile, ring, no ring.

Great Dogs of History

Rin Tin Tin, of course, and Lassie,
and the nameless dogs, the ones
at the edge of paintings, at the edge

of a child's mind before it goes to sleep,
at the edge of a child's painting
on the fridge door. The dog that howled

and woke Jesus up in his manger
but he never cried and just looked,
smiling, at the gifts the men brought,

the men at the edge of the picture.
The faithful dog who waited for years
beside his master's grave, because

his master said he had gone for food
and the master is always right
listen to his voice, at the edge

of the fridge. The dog who brought
news of the deaths of all those
people, all those people

and he never cried and just looked,
and this dog and that dog and
the paw prints at the edge of the fridge

and this dog. Woof. This dog. Bark.
Oh, Lassie of course, and Rin Tin Tin,
barking. The men at the edge of the picture.

The Veins in my Neck

Sunset in Howell Wood;
midwinter sunset
like a fire going out.

The veins in my neck
stand out like drainpipes
when I'm angry.

Look at my dad in this photo
holding a fish
as big as himself.

It's a life, this.
Look at it. It's
a life in sunsets,

sunsets and fish.
Midwinter sunsets
like fires going out.

Black against red,
headgear and sky.
If it was a sound

it would be the sound
a burning tree makes
in heavy rain.

Migrations and exiles,
pithead to pithead,
Ayrshire to Yorkshire

like fires going out;
sunset, smoke,
midwinter drainpipes

as big as himself.
Lots of men in this wood
walking babies and children.

Midwinter sunset,
time on your hands
like a fish

as big as yourself,
a fire going out,
a life in sunsets.

Beethoven was Deaf, You Know

Recently there have been
two car chases round Darfield
in the early early hours.

During one car chase
I was pissing in a bus shelter
and I didn't hear the car chase
but they heard me pissing.

Car chase.

Car
chase.

You stand the words on top of each other.
Make a little tower.
Such a modern thing, a car chase.

Fact: Shakespeare could not have written about a

car
chase.

It's too modern.

But a car chase
that you can't hear.
How modern is that?

'Many of McMillan's poems
take place at night'
Because most of your life
takes place at night.

Here, chase this.
It's only a toy
but it works.
Wind it up.
Make a little tower
Such a modern thing, a machine,

a poem, a car
chase.

In a West Yorkshire Bus Queue,
Several Mature Art Students Discuss Excitedly
the Earthquake of April 2nd 1990

I was leaning against the wall,
phoning my husband/a present from
Polperro, it just fell to the ground,
drifted like a leaf. The light
in St Ives/he works in Oldham and he said

Yes, Yes, I can feel it too!

I was in my studio, well I call it/
I ran out onto the lawn to stand,
to experience it and well, my dear,
I had quite forgotten, quite forgotten

that I was naked!

my studio, it's really the shed.
The paints ran, I swear the paints
ran down the canvas/ at first

I covered my breasts!

I'm working on a new piece,
two people, leaning against walls,
miles apart!

November 1963 in
a Scotland of the Mind

The milkman is framed
in the glass door.

John Kennedy is dressing
to be shot

again and again
in films for ever,

later. The milkman
is holding

a Scottish pound note
for my dad

the village's one
Scotsman.

Jock, they call him.
It isn't his name.

Upstairs, he is dressing,
pulling on his trousers

singing an Andy Stewart
song, probably

Donald Where's Yer Troosers,
I think.

The Making of the English Working Class

George dreams of silence.
Isobel sleeps in the wash house.
Olive weeps in hedges.

Alice sprains her wrist polishing.
Harry writes to his wife.
Charlie drives someone's car into town.

Arthur can't hear what you say.
Doris can't find her finger.
Henry is laughed at.

Sammy feels his neck breaking.
Danny falls overboard.
Jacky stares at nothing.

Tommy sees his arm in the machine.
Jimmy walks to Rochdale.
Nelly coughs in her room.

Eddie can't move.
Barry vomits into a scarf.
Annie looks up at the roof fall.

Billy has lost the use of his legs.
Sally has scars an inch deep.
Willy dribbles down his cardigan.